Principles-Based Planning

A Better Approach to Financial Planning

Kyle J Christensen, CFP®

ISBN: 979-8-6651-3231-0

DEDICATION

In gratitude to my wife, Amber, who is the light and inspiration of my life. To each of my three children, who give greater meaning to my life than anything else. To my parents and church leaders, who taught me vital principles of life and happiness.

I love you all.

DISCLAIMER

This book is designed to provide accurate information in regard to the subject matter covered at the time of publication. It is published with the understanding that the author is not engaged in rendering legal, accounting, financial, or other professional service. If legal or financial advice or other expert assistance is required, the services of a competent professional should be sought.

TABLE OF CONTENTS

Principles-Based Planning
A Better Approach to Financial Planning

Introduction

Like many Americans today, I grew up in a home where my parents were divorced. This happened when I was two years old. Most of my growing up years were spent living with my dad, which was unusual for the time, and even today. Most kids end up with their mom in a divorce. Although the situation of my growing up was not as anyone would have planned, it caused me to grow up quicker, to learn important lessons that still bless my life today. I believe that through difficulty we often learn our most valuable lessons.

I started my adult life by serving a two-year mission for my church and my God. I dedicated every moment of every day for those two years to serving the wonderful people of Brazil. Between high school and the time I started my mission I worked and saved as much money as I could so that I could pay for my mission. This is something most missionaries in our church do. If the missionary himself/herself doesn't pay for their own mission, usually parents or other family members do. On my mission I learned the true meaning of hard work and sacrifice. Serving in Brazil was a great blessing for many reasons. One blessing was that I was able to recognize how fortunate we are to live in the United States and the incredible opportunities that living here affords us. Most people that are born into poverty in places like Brazil, have no chance of getting out of it on their own. As I served my mission I also learned the value of thinking of others first instead of myself. I discovered that this was the big "secret" to true happiness.

After returning home from my mission I started my college education at Utah State University. At first, I wanted to become a physical therapist. I loved playing and being in and around athletics, so I figured this would be a career choice that would give me that opportunity. I also wanted a career where I would work one on one with people to help them achieve their goals. Not long into my college career I met and started dating the love of my life. She and I got married just after my freshman year.

Sometime around my third year of college a former church youth leader of mine stopped and talked with me at the grocery store where

1

I was working while going to school. He helped me recall a conversation we had prior to my serving a mission. In that conversation I had asked him what he did for a living. He was a great leader. He inspired and taught me so much. I admired that he could go to most of the youths' sporting events and activities to support them. I admired that he was able to spend so much time with his own family. I recognized that he made a good living and wasn't as stressed financially as most of the people I knew, including my parents. I recognized that most adults worked for money. Their jobs dictated their lives, what they could do, when they could do it, and so on.

I didn't want that to be my future. I wanted to be in control of my life, in control of my time. I knew that being successful financially was how I would be able to do it. Mistakenly, I thought, at the time, that it was all about the career I would choose and how much money I would make. I've since discovered that it's not how much money a person makes as much as it what they do with what they make that makes the difference.

When my former youth church leader spoke with me in the grocery store that day he asked me, "Kyle, do you still want to know what I do?" At the time I was working in the meat department of the grocery store making somewhere around $7 per hour. Needless to say, I was open to almost any job ideas. My wife and I scheduled a time to meet with him to find out more about what he did for a living.

That meeting in 1999 was my introduction to the world of financial services. I was very interested to learn more, and began my own journey to learn how money really works. I found myself reading all kinds of books on finances. One of the first was *Rich Dad Poor Dad*, by Robert Kiyosaki. The things he said struck a chord with me. I believed him. I believed what he was saying because I had witnessed so many people "working for money" and not the other way around. I could see that most people were not on a path to financial freedom. Most were slaves to money. I didn't want my life to be like that. I knew that following the crowd was going to lead me to the same place the crowd was going, and that wasn't where I wanted to be.

As I pursued this course I discovered that I loved finances. I loved learning about finances, and I loved teaching about finances. I loved helping people, one on one, with intimate and important decisions. I came to realize that this is what I wanted to do for a living.

After that I decided to take all of the required courses to be able to sit for the CERTIFIED FINANCIAL PLANNER™ exam. Luckily, Utah State University was one of the few universities in the state that was accredited by the CFP Board. I took the necessary courses, and in 2003 sat for and passed the CFP® exam. There were two purposes for me becoming certified. First, I was only 23 years old when I began in the industry. I thought, "Why would any 50+ year old want to talk with me? Why would they give me any credibility?" The CFP® designation gave me that credibility. Second, I simply wanted to learn and become an expert. One of the downsides of this industry, and one of the reasons people are skeptical about meeting with "financial advisors" is the fact that no formal education is required. A person can simply get licensed and start advising. No prior experience or education necessary.

Robert Kiyosaki, in his most recent book, *Fake: Fake Money, Fake Teachers, Fake Assets*, puts it this way:

> Most of today's 30-Day Wonder financial planners know little to nothing about investing. They study only to pass a Series 7 [and I would add, and/or only to pass an insurance license].
>
> The difference between a 30-Day Wonder and a CFP is much like the difference between a bookkeeper and a CPA.
>
> After a 30-Day Wonder receives their license, they hit the streets looking for clients. Most are looking for a person who is unhappy with their current financial planner. The new planner then convinces the unhappy customer to switch the "assets" in his 401(k) or IRA over to him, and he will make the magic happen. Most of the time, the magic doesn't happen. How can there be much magic? All financial planners are selling basically the same

products: stocks, bonds, mutual funds, ETF's, savings, and insurance.

Magic does not happen because the name of the game financial planning companies play is *not* "Make our clients rich." The game financial planning companies play is "assets under management," or AUM.

I became a CFP® in 2003 and started my own financial planning practice in 2004. Becoming a CFP® gives me expert insight as to what traditional financial planning teaches and promotes. My planning practice is not focused on AUM. My planning practice is focused on helping clients become "rich," or as I like to call it, financially free. The purpose of this book is to show the difference in the philosophy that helps people actually become financially free, versus the common advice that is being promoted by the crowd and followed by the crowd.

Part I: Principles-Based Planning: The Best Approach

Chapter 1 – Principles – Our Inner Compass

What are principles?

How do principles affect daily decision-making?

How do principles help people choose among the myriad of choices they make throughout their lives?

Principles have been proven over time, and in any circumstance, to always lead to a desirable long-term result. People learn principles by observing others, through study, and by their own experiences. As people discover, prove, and learn to trust their principles, those principles can become a guide for making decisions.

Synonyms for the word principle are precept, rule, standard, or tenet. For me, a principle is something that I follow, regardless of my circumstance or situation.

The world around me changes, but my principles do not. I hold tight to important principles in my life. They are a guide. They help me make sense of the world, and they help guide my decisions.

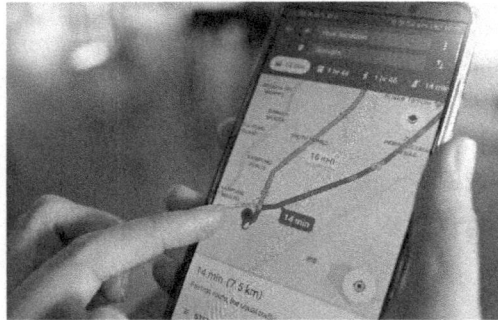

A good principle is one that never fails. It is like an accurate map and compass. With a map and a compass I can find my way safely to my destination.

In the book *The Seven Habits of Highly Successful People*, Stephen R. Covey starts out by talking about Paradigms and Principles. He states, "The Character Ethic taught that there are basic principles of effective living, and that people can only experience true success and enduring happiness as they learn and integrate these principles into their basic character."

Mr. Covey is stating that he discovered some important and vital principles, related to life, that are vital to the achievement of enduring happiness and what he calls "true success."

His book, *The Seven Habits of Highly Successful People* lay out what those principles are. Does Mr. Covey need to predict the future to help people maximize the happiness in their lives? Absolutely not! What he can do, and has done, is provide people with foundational principles to live by, to help guide their decisions throughout their lives.

Does this type of planning work? Ask the millions upon millions of people who have read his books and implemented Mr. Covey's principles. It works. If you have not read his book, I highly recommend it. It will help you, and it will help you know how to help your clients in a better way.

True principles are not circumstantial. True principles stand the test of time, are applicable in any situation, and at any stage in life.

By contrast, objectives may change, and are likely to change, based on circumstances or stage in life. For example, as a principle, I am always going to save some of the money I earn. However, what I am saving for may change. Saving is the principle, and what I am saving for is the objective.

Ray Dalio points out in his book *Principles: Life and Work*, that "All successful people operate by principles that help them be successful..."

"Principles," Mr. Dalio says, "are fundamental truths that serve as the foundations for behavior that gets you what you want out of life. They can be applied again and again in similar situations to help you achieve your goals...Without principles we would be forced to react to all the things life throws at us individually, as if we were experiencing each of them for the first time."

Two of the principles that affect how I make my decisions are honesty and hard work.

The Principle of Honesty

When one of my daughters was about five years old, we went into a farm and ranch store to see the baby chicks and ducklings they were selling.

After we were done, we walked out of the store and got into the truck. I then looked back and saw one of my daughters holding a small toy animal. I didn't recognize it as something we owned.

I asked her where she got it. She looked a little sheepish and knew that she had done something wrong. She finally confessed that she saw it in the store and put it in her pocket.

My wife and I talked with her about the importance of being honest and not stealing. We told her she had to go back in the store and tell the store owner what happened and give back the toy. It was an emotional and an embarrassing event for her, but it engrained in her the principle of honesty.

Personal integrity and being trustworthy are some of the results of being honest.

One of the most precious and valuable characteristics of an individual is his or her personal integrity. Integrity is built by always telling the truth.

I remember the story *The Boy Who Cried Wolf* that I read and heard many times as a child. In the story there was a town of people who were sheep herders. They hired children to watch over their sheep at night. The children watching over the sheep were told to yell, "Wolf!" if they ever saw a wolf come near the sheep, and if they yelled wolf, the people would come running to scare off the wolf.

One day one of the boys watching over the sheep thought it would be funny to yell "Wolf!" even though there wasn't a wolf around. He just wanted to see the reaction of the people. So, he yelled "Wolf!" and sure enough the townspeople came running to scare off the wolf and save the herd of sheep. When they got there, there was no wolf in sight. The townspeople asked the boy if he saw a wolf, and he swore that there was one, even though he knew it was a lie.

The boy repeated this a few more times, and as he did so the people started to wonder if he was simply making things up. They started to distrust him.

Illustration by Katie M. Christensen

Eventually a real wolf did show up to attack the sheep. The boy cried "Wolf!", but this time no one responded. The people didn't believe the boy anymore. The wolf slaughtered the sheep. The next day the townspeople came to check on their sheep and they were all dead.

That story, along with lessons on honesty that I learned from my parents and reinforced by my church, helped me understand and adopt the principle of honesty as a young child.

In Stephen M.R. Covey's book, *The Speed of Trust*, we learn that trust leads to increased productivity and decreased trust has a tangible cost in the realm of business. I believe that decreased trust creates a cost in all aspects of a person's life. Even if a person does as much research as possible about an important choice, trust is ultimately how decisions are made. Trust is why a person decides either to work with you or not.

The financial services industry has garnered a lot of distrust from the public because too many in our industry have been willing to tell a lie in order to make money.

They choose money over maintaining integrity. If you want longevity in this business and inner peace in your own life, always tell the truth, even if it means you don't make the sale. Many things are more important than money. Your integrity is one of them.

The Principle of Work

When I was a little boy my dad was my hero. I wanted to be just like him. The one thing that stood out to me more than any other trait was that my dad worked hard.

I had the privilege of going with him in his sales truck to visit farmers all over northern Utah and southern Idaho. I was amazed at his energy and enthusiasm. It seemed like he was friends with every farmer. They knew him and he knew them.

There were many times that we would be driving on a dusty dirt road in the country and suddenly my dad would stop the truck, jump out and grab a drink out of the cooler in the bed of the truck, hop the fence and run out to the farmer in the field. My dad would climb into the tractor cab, have a quick chat with the farmer, and give him a nice cold drink.

On days when my dad was at the farm implement store I got to see him work with customers as they came in, needing this part or that. I saw him pull out these gigantic binders or catalogs, full of thousands of numbers for every farm equipment part they made. He was quick. He knew most of the numbers by heart. I was amazed.

Whenever there was a lull at the store my dad could be found organizing or improving how things were displayed, researching parts, and solving problems. He didn't want me standing around idly either, so he always had jobs for me to do. I swept the parking lot and the aisles in the store, cleaned up the break room, refilled the pop machines (which was my favorite because he always gave me a free pop), I didn't earn any money from those jobs. I was just excited to be working with my dad and learning from him. I learned that working hard had its own internal rewards.

My dad didn't just work hard at work, he also worked hard at home. For example, we used to heat our home with a wood burning stove and therefore we needed to go up in the mountains and get firewood every Fall. This was hard work, especially for an eight or nine year-old kid!

Illustration by Katie M. Christensen

My dad would fell the trees with a chainsaw and then cut them into smaller pieces that could be chopped for firewood. Mine and my brothers' job was to gather the cut pieces of wood, haul them down and load them in our white 1968 Ford truck.

I'm not sure how many cords of wood we loaded into the truck each trip, but all I can say is that it was a miraculous amount. It was extremely hard work, but I learned to love it.

My Grandma told me about a time when I was little and she asked me what I wanted to be when I grew up. She said my response was, "I want to be a hard worker like my dad".

From my dad I learned the principle of hard work. From playing sports I learned that hard work oftentimes was more valuable than talent. In college I learned that through hard work I could get really good grades and more importantly learn important information. In business I have learned that through hard work I can support and serve my family.

I have learned that through hard work I can accomplish almost anything I want in this life. This principle has guided me throughout my life and has blessed me in countless ways.

It is interesting to me how many people want to create wealth, but don't want to work hard to do it.

To me that's like trying to make chocolate chip cookies without putting in the chocolate chips.

Work is a necessary ingredient to success. It is a foundational principle of success. Those who want to avoid work will eventually lose because they are trying to violate that principle. In Robert Kiyosaki's book, _Fake_, he says "Getting rich takes work and discipline." Ultimately, no long-term enduring success comes without work.

If principles work in our personal lives and in business, wouldn't it make sense that they work in financial planning as well? Brian Tracy taught that, "Success leaves tracks." To be successful in any area of life you simply need to study what successful people have done and do what they did. Luckily, we have research and best practices recorded by some of the most successful people in personal finance, including Warren Buffet, Robert Kiyosaki, Kim Butler, Napoleon Hill, Dr. Thomas Stanley, and others.

I have made it my mission to study and evaluate what successful and unsuccessful people have done. What I have found is that the all highly successful people follow true principles, which they use to evaluate their decisions, including their financial decisions.

Unfortunately, the majority of people do not have or follow any real financial principles. They are sold false ideas in the guise of being financial principles, even though those ideas are anything but. Those false ideas are packaged together in a process called Financial-Needs Analysis and the Accumulation Theory (neither of which are followed by the most successful people and financial institutions), by the financial planning community. Even though the evidence is clear that the method being promoted to the masses does not work, most financial planners continue to push it.

Why would the financial planning community push something that doesn't work and continuously falls short? Convenience and Ease are two of the reasons. Financial needs analysis and the accumulation method are easy and convenient, and most financial planners have never been shown a different way. You simply hand the client a questionnaire, feed the answers into your software program with

12

assumptions the client is supposed to know, and out comes a 200-page financial plan with lots of fancy charts and graphs.

Some of those assumptions include what age they will retire at, how long they will live, what their rate of return will be, what inflation will be, and how much money they will need at retirement. Unfortunately, we do not know the answer to any of those questions with any degree of certainty, which makes building a financial plan on top of those assumptions a shaky proposition.

Ease and convenience have rarely produced positive enduring results. There is a better way, and that is to follow time-tested principles.

Principles are the way we make important decisions in our lives. They are our guide and our foundation. Principles-based planning is the most effective way to approach financial planning and the most beneficial to the client.

We will explore principles-based planning in Part III of this book.

First, though we need to look at Financial Needs Analysis and the Accumulation Theory to see why they do not work.

Part II: Financial Needs Analysis and the Accumulation Theory

Chapter 2: Financial-Needs Analysis

Financial Needs Analysis (FNA) began in the 1970s as a means of marketing and selling financial products to consumers. The idea behind Financial Needs Analysis was that if the advisor could demonstrate a "need" to the client, he/she would be more motivated to buy the product the advisor was recommending.

FNA was in contrast to simply showing a client what the advisor was promoting as a better tool or product, or simply trying to convince the client to save or invest more money or purchase more insurance coverage.

This new sales tactic required an amount of complexity in order to demonstrate the proposed need. Over time FNA has become more and more complex as more and more variables have been added to the "analysis." Various factors such as taxes, inflation, rates of return, and even various "real-life" scenarios can be played out in projections of the future (i.e. Monte Carlo Simulations).

This complexity has been added to make it look more real to the client, to try to get the client to feel like they are actually in the scenario being laid out, or that it is a real prediction of their financial future.

There are many financial planning software programs that will produce or calculate hundreds (maybe even thousands) of scenarios and give the client different percentages for likelihood for success or failure based on each scenario. These scenarios can even draw in "historical returns" from the market itself (various indexes or possibly even specific funds).

The software comes up with the plan, what to do, and recommendations for where to invest.. The advisor can have an influence on what the program spits out, but it can also be pretty automated, with built-in biases and pre-determined direction for clients.

With all of this complexity that has been added to needs-based analysis, and the incredible calculations that can be made using powerful and complicated software, there is only one absolute truth about the projections and the pre-determined "needs" they create, and that is that the projections and predictions of what the clients need are all wrong.

There is almost 100% certainty that the projections of the future are not actually going to play out the way they are being shown to clients. There is almost 100% certainty that the "real life" scenarios that the financial planners arbitrarily put into these systems are not going to be what actually happens.

The sad part about FNA is that most financial planners who use it in their planning, actually believe that it's right. They have forgotten that FNA was and is only a means of selling financial products. FNA is a sales tactic! The really sad part about FNA is that clients have been trained to believe that financial planners and advisors, or that they themselves can predict the future using this method.

For example, consider the question often asked by financial planners:

"How much money do you think you need to live on in retirement?"

How would a client know the answer to that question? Unless they can predict the future, they can't give you the right answer!

Financial Needs Analysis is not actually a real way to predict clients' future needs.

No one can do it.

No program can do it.

No software can predict the future needs of an individual and his/her family. None of us can actually know, with any amount of certainty, what is going to happen in the lives of our clients over the years to come. Nor can we predict which investments will perform best, what their rates of return will be, what taxes or inflation will be, what laws are going to remain, and which ones are going to change.

The only thing that is certain is change.

Your clients' lives will change. Their desires will change. The investments that exist today may go away entirely, and new ones will come along (i.e. Roth IRA's did not exist prior to 1998).

Laws have changed, and they can, and will, continue to change over time.

Taxes have changed, and they can, and will, continue to change over time.

The stock market will not "repeat itself." I'll give you two examples of why:

1) The internet didn't always exist. Talk about one thing that completely changed the market! Has it had a major influence on the market? Absolutely! Will something else come along that completely changes the market (for good or bad)? YES. Of course. Do we know what it is? No.

2) There are significantly more people/businesses getting pieces of the stock market pie now than there were in the 1950's and 60's. Watch *The Retirement Gamble* (documentary on PBS Frontline). Even Warren Buffet says the market will not repeat itself because of this factor alone. Read his article entitled, *Cut Your Gains* (Fortune, March 20, 2006).

Change is going to happen, and it is not predictable how, when, or what. You cannot predict your clients' futures and you cannot predict what the stock market or any investment market is going to do.

While Financial Needs Analysis has been successful for decades <u>for financial institutions and financial advisors</u>, helping them sell and position their products, it has fallen short at helping clients achieve their full potential in their individual finances. It has also created a huge amount of dependence on consumer debt, Social Security, and other government programs.

How is the average American family doing with the Financial Needs Analysis approach?

Most Americans are underinsured when it comes to life insurance, and they know it.

Most Americans do not have adequate disability insurance protection, and unfortunately, very few advisors bring up the issue.

Most Americans do not have adequate liability insurance on their homes or cars, and the education they receive from their P&C agents or financial planners is little to non-existent.

Most Americans do not have their estate planning completed, nor do they know why they should.

Most Americans are far from having enough money in their liquid income storage for emergencies, layoffs, career moves, or the unexpected. Liquidity is not a major focus for most advisors.

Most Americans are far from being able to replace their earned income with income from investment assets when they reach normal retirement age (even though most retire anyway and become totally dependent on Social Security and welfare). The 2018 Retirement Confidence Survey (EBRI) reports that 67% of retirees say that Social Security is a major source of retirement income for them.

Too many Americans are overburdened with debt. Too many Americans have to borrow funds from their qualified retirement plans because of a lack of liquidity reserved for unpredictable situations in their lives.

Too many Americans are heading into retirement still owing money on their primary residence. About 44% of Americans age 60-70 still have a mortgage (according to the Washington Post 03/22/2018).

What we should be asking ourselves in our industry is whether or not the philosophy we are promoting is contributing to these terrible statistics. I believe it is. I believe needs-based analysis and our love affair with the stock market and the accumulation theory has come at a high price for the general public.

Here are a few recent charts and headlines for articles supporting what I've stated:

Life insurance: How to make sure you're not underinsured

Satta Sarmah-Hightower - Last updated: Feb. 26, 2020

Only 59 percent of Americans have life insurance, and about half of those with insurance are underinsured, according to LIMRA.

Many Retired People Don't Expect to Pay Off Mortgages

Survey finds that 44 percent of Americans are still paying for their home when they retire

by Kim Hayes, AARP, March 26, 2018 | 💬 Comments: 9

PERSONAL FINANCE · Published January 22

Most Americans can't afford an unexpected $1,000 expense, study finds

About 16% of adults say they'd finance it with a credit card and pay it off over time

By Megan Henney | FOXBusiness

Markets
Market data delayed at least 15 minutes

Figure 1. Life insurance ownership

percentage of households with life insurance

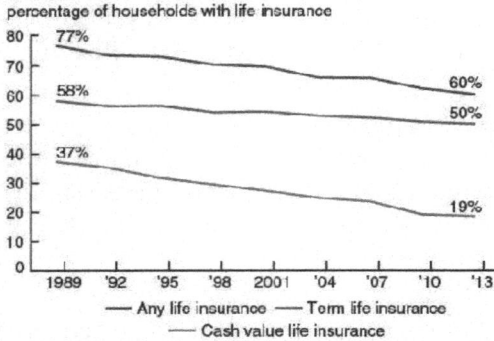

— Any life insurance — Term life insurance
— Cash value life insurance

Notes: All observations have been weighted to reflect the U.S. population and all dollar values have been adjusted to 2013 dollars. The sample observations are made up of those aged 18-75.
Source: Authors' calculations based on data from the Board of Governors of the Federal Reserve System *Survey of Consumer Finances.*

Percent of U.S. Workers with Disability Coverage Declines

June 8, 2011

Email This   Subscribe to Newsletter

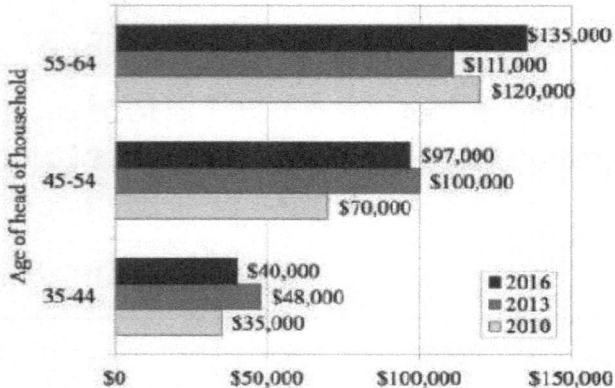

FIGURE 10. MEDIAN 401(K)/IRA BALANCES OF WORKING HOUSEHOLDS WITH 401(K)S BY AGE, 2010, 2013, AND 2016

Note: Sample excludes households that are not working and those that have only an IRA.

20

To what extent (do you expect/is) each of the following (to be) a source of income in retirement?
Workers who plan to retire or have retired n=904; Retirees n=1,040

Social Security

Workers

86%
Major/Minor
Source

13%

36%

50%

- Major Source
- Minor Source
- Not a Source

Retirees

91%
Major/Minor
Source

8%

24%

67%

The word "need" is synonymous with the word minimum, or the amount that is absolutely necessary in order to survive. To have only what you need is to have the minimum you need.

Need and Maximum are very different from one another. Do you think needs or minimums are what motivates people?

If you had the choice of creating a financial plan that would give you much less than you have today, give you much less financial freedom, and would only provide you with the necessities of life, would you choose that?

Would you be more motivated to choose a plan that strives to maximize your future wealth and freedom, to whatever that number might be (without predictions)?

If you had a plan that was designed to strive for maximum, but fell somewhere short of that, would you be better or worse off than if you had a plan where the target was your minimum need and you fell short on that?

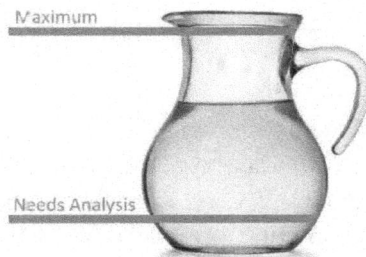

Maximum

Needs Analysis

Therein lies one of the major problems with needs-based planning. Where is the room for error? Where is the room for change? Where is the room for unplanned life events?

If you were getting on an airplane to go somewhere, and the captain of the flight turned on the radio and said, "I just want you to know that we have exactly the amount of fuel we need for the trip, and nothing extra" what would you do? Would you buckle your seat belt and stay on the plane, or would you get off? Do airplanes carry more fuel than they believe is necessary for the trip? Of course they do! It may not be a lot extra, but they do carry extra.

For another example, when you look at weather forecasts, which ones do you take the most seriously? Which ones are the most accurate? Are the forecasts of temperatures next week or this week more accurate? Are the forecasts of what is going to happen today more accurate than the forecast for the coming weekend?

NEXT 36 HOURS   HOURLY → | 10 DAYS →

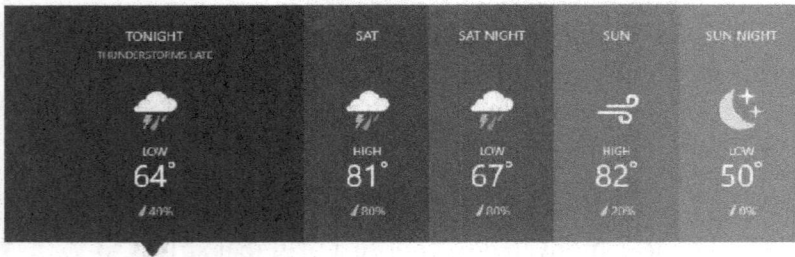

TONIGHT THUNDERSTORMS LATE	SAT	SAT NIGHT	SUN	SUN NIGHT
LOW 64°	HIGH 81°	LOW 67°	HIGH 82°	LOW 50°
40%	80%	80%	20%	0%

The further out the forecast is, the more likely it is to be wrong. In fact, according to the National Oceanic and Atmospheric Administration a seven-day forecast is accurate about 80% of time, whereas a ten-day or longer forecast is only accurate about half of the time.

The same is true when it comes to finances. The further out we are trying to predict something, the more likely we will be wrong. The difference is, we are not talking about the weather. We are talking about someone's financial life, which is usually much more serious.

One of the principles we focus on is Maximum. Whenever we talk about maximum, in almost any setting, it forces us to focus on efficiency.

What is efficiency? Something that is efficient is something that has minimal or no loss or waste.

For example, I ran track in high school, and I took courses in exercise science in college. One of the things that you would think everyone knows how to do is how to run, right? Everyone knows how to do that don't they? Nope. I have watched my kids play sports enough to know that there are many kids who don't know how to run properly. There are also plenty of adults who never learned how to run properly.

There is technique to running. Running efficiently allows you to conserve energy. Running efficiently minimizes wasted energy. Because winning races in track events (especially sprints) is usually a difference of a split second, the person who has the best combination of strength, speed, and efficiency usually wins.

Why is efficiency in finances important? If you had unlimited resources (unlimited money supply) then efficiency would not matter, but we do have limited resources. Our clients have limited resources. That is one of the reasons they are meeting with you!

If losing money was not a problem, they would not need you at all. One of our major objectives as we work with clients is to help them identify where money is being lost or is being used inefficiently.

If you gave one person a bucket with no holes in it, and another person a bucket with holes all over it, and asked them to each fill up the bucket, which one would fill it up the fastest (assuming the same water supply and pressure)? It's pretty obvious. What would be the best advice to the individual with the hole-filled bucket? Would it be to find more ways to put more water into the bucket or increase the water pressure from the hose? Of course not. The best advice would be for him to find ways to plug the holes in the bucket and make his bucket more efficient.

What advice does traditional financial planning give regarding efficiency? Not much. The answer given by most financial advisors is not to find the "financial leaks" and plug them. The advice given is simply to add more water.

Americans Not Saving Enough, But Resolve to Do Better in 2020

New survey from Principal shows "not saving enough" remains the biggest financial blunder, but 21% say they will resolve to save more for retirement in 2020

Posted by Brian Anderson — December 3, 2019   In Financial Wellness, Principal, Your 401k News   💬 0

Granted, Americans, for the most part really are not saving enough, but very few advisors are finding out why. They are just telling their clients they "need" to save more. They aren't helping them find ways to reduce and recapture costs. They show their clients how much they've saved, and where they "need" to be (their retirement goal), and the "gap" (how much more money they're going to need in order to reach the goal, based on a myriad of assumptions that cannot be predicted—although they pretend to be able to predict).

A focus on reducing, eliminating, and recapturing money that would otherwise be wasted should be one of our main objectives as advisors.

In general, people have much more control over efficiency than they do over rates of return on investments. Think of the places people lose money over their lifetimes, including insurance premiums, taxes, fees, and inflation.

Let's take a married couple, both 37 years old, with two small children, who make about $100,000 per year in income, living somewhere in the Midwest. Let's say they have a modest home and two vehicles. Just for insurance coverage they are probably going to be spending around $7,700 per year ($1,500 auto, $1,200 homeowners, $4,000 medical, $1,000 life insurance & disability insurance).

For income and property taxes (which are just a few of the many taxes we pay), they are probably going to be spending around $15,600 per year ($9,600 federal income taxes, $4,000 state income taxes, and $2,000 property taxes).

Let's assume the couple has an IRA with a brokerage firm that charges them 1% per year on a balance of $200,000. Additionally, their mutual funds also charge management fees and costs associated with the funds and their underlying investments at a rate of 1% (which is far below the average costs of actively managed funds). In total they are paying $4,000 per year in investment management fees. If we add insurance, investment fees and taxes together, they are paying a total of $27,300 per year.

Compare this to the amount of money they are saving and investing for retirement. Most likely they aren't saving more than 10% of their total income, which is $10,000 per year.

Which area do they have more control and influence? Increasing their rate of return on their investments or finding ways to recover or reduce their costs associated with insurance, taxes, and fees?

The client has zero control or influence on the rate of return on his portfolio of mutual funds in his IRA. Over this client's lifetime, they are going to spend more than $819,000 in taxes, insurance, and fees, compared to the $300,000 they will save/invest over the same timeframe.

It is clear that we, as advisors, should make the principles of efficiency and cost recovery a major focus of our planning.

Chapter 3: The Accumulation Theory

There really are only two major philosophies when it comes to wealth creation. The most popular one is The Accumulation Theory. This is the theory that the large majority of financial professionals use for planning purposes. This is also the theory that is adopted by most universities, financial planning organizations, financial institutions and financial talking heads, including people like Dave Ramsey and Suze Orman.

I call the other major philosophy The Velocity of Money Method. Although this method is not talked about as often in the public arena, this method has created the most millionaires and billionaires throughout the history of the United States and is supported by authors such as Kim Butler, Robert Kiyosaki, Napoleon Hill, and Thomas Stanley.

Before I go into detail on these two major philosophies, I think it is important to establish what all financial institutions want.

1. They want our money.
2. They want our money on a regular and ongoing basis.
3. They want to keep our money for as long as possible.
4. They want to give back as little as possible.

This all makes sense, right? If you owned a bank and I was your customer, what would you want me to do? Probably all of the things we just listed.

To achieve their goals, financial institutions promote products and strategies, such as the accumulation of assets. They do this by encouraging things like building a retirement nest egg, living on the interest only of that nest egg, self-insuring in retirement, and so on.

They encourage advisors and even congratulate and award financial advisors based on how much money they accumulate as "assets under management."

The amount of assets under management gives a financial institution bragging rights and power in the industry. Goldman Sachs, for example, has more than $1 trillion in assets under management. That's more wealth than New Zealand, Turkey, Saudi Arabia, and hundreds of other countries have in their entireties.

We also benefit from financial institutions. They can create products and provide guarantees and benefits that we otherwise could not get on our own. With that said, it is extremely important, in the context of wealth-building, to know what their intentions are, and how they may or may not align with ours.

Accumulation of assets is obviously and blatantly the goal of advisors subscribing to the Accumulation Method, and it is exactly what the financial institutions they work for want them to do.

There is a major conflict of interest for accumulation theory advisors (specifically those who are paid a percentage based on the investment assets they manage). If their clients pull money out of the accounts to use or live on, the advisor receives less income.

There is a negative financial consequence to the advisor if the client withdraws some money. This is indisputable. Even if a financial advisor is a fee-based advisor, the brokerage that houses the investment funds definitely has a conflict of interest regarding the client using his/her money at any point.

Because of this, advisors talk about "compounding interest", "reinvesting dividends", and so forth. They encourage this because they really do not want the investor to take money out of the account. If dividends are automatically reinvested, the advisor and/or the brokerage can charge more fees.

Don't you think it is important for a client to know that investment advisors and asset managers have a vested interest in them never using their money?

Sometimes as we go through the planning process and we give a client a recommendation that they either haven't heard of, or they know isn't popular, they will ask something like this, "This seems really great Kyle, but why haven't I heard of this before?" or "This looks almost too good to be true. Why aren't more people doing it?" or "So and so (i.e. Dave Ramsey) says that this is a terrible product. Why is he so much against it?"

Those are valid questions for a client to ask. They have been inundated with marketing their entire adult lives, even from the time they were in college (i.e. White Coat Investor, The Wealthy Barber, the investment professor, etc.).

Is it possible that what is popular is popular by design? Is it possible that the things that we hear about the most, when it comes to financial advice, are promoted by none other than the financial institutions themselves? Why? There can only be one reason, and it is not because they are concerned about our well-being. It is because what they are promoting helps them accomplish the goals they have with our money. It is in the financial institutions' best interests.

The accumulation theory is based on a few main ideas.

First, is the idea that we can, supposedly, predict the future, including future rates of return based on risk tolerance, asset allocation, duration of the plan, the client's future situation and circumstances, and so on.

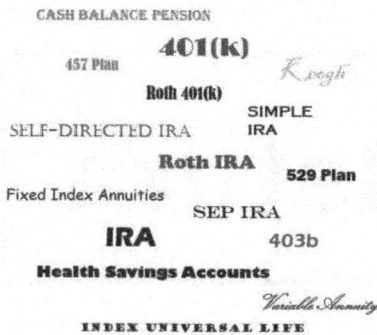

CASH BALANCE PENSION
401(k)
457 Plan
Keogh
Roth 401(k)
SIMPLE IRA
SELF-DIRECTED IRA
Roth IRA
529 Plan
Fixed Index Annuities
SEP IRA
IRA   403b
Health Savings Accounts
Variable Annuity
INDEX UNIVERSAL LIFE

Second, the stock market is the foundational basis for the success of every plan. Everything rides on it. If the stock market does not work as predicted, the entire plan fails. As a result of the stock market being the foundation of the plan, as much money as possible needs to be invested in the market to ensure success.

Third, is the idea of "building a nest egg" that is large enough that a person or couple can retire and live on the interest or income from it for the rest of his/her life. That is why we hear advertising that asks you if you "know your number," which is supposedly the amount of money you have to accumulate in order to be able to retire.

Some of the terminology and strategies associated with the Accumulation Theory of wealth building are:

- Retirement Nest egg
- Compounding interest
- Dollar-Cost Averaging
- Asset Allocation

- Diversification
- Self-insurance
- Risk Tolerance testing
- Monte Carlo Simulations
- The Rule of 72
- Average Rates of Return
- 401(k)'s
- IRA's
- 529 Plans
- Qualified Plans
- Employer Match
- Retirement savings
- Risk equals reward
- Buy and hold and more.

Risk = Return

We'll address many of these individually.

The overall theory is this: You work and earn, "save" some of what you earn into investments, typically mutual funds in all their varieties (ETF's, SPDR's, Index Funds, actively managed funds, REIT's, hedge funds, etc.).

They use the word "save" instead of "invest" because saving sounds safer than investing. The goal, according to this philosophy, is to save (or invest) at all times, regardless of what the price of the stock or mutual fund is.

The process of *always buying* is called "Dollar-Cost Averaging." To make this sound like a good thing, they tell clients that you cannot predict when the right time to buy is, so you should *always* buy.

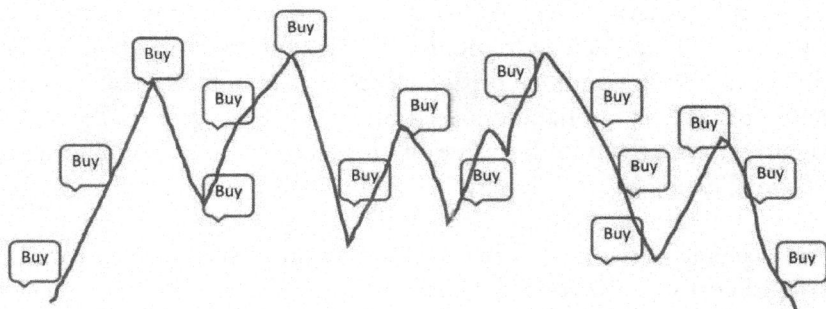

Dollar-Cost Averaging

Using this strategy, admittedly, you will buy some shares when they are high, but you will also buy shares when the price is low, and over time it all averages out.

Usually the investments are held inside IRA's and qualified plans (i.e. 401(k)'s). You "diversify" your funds, so that you don't have "all your eggs in one basket". What this means is that you put your money into a myriad of funds that are spread across a wide array of investment classes and fields (i.e. oil and gas, tech, health, pharmaceutical, emerging markets, US large companies, small companies, and so on).

Your investments are then supposed to "compound" in interest over time, which advisors often refer to as a "miracle".

Interestingly no investments actually compound interest. They either appreciate or depreciate. Yes, some pay dividends or interest, and yes, investment firms do encourage you to reinvest those dividends and interest, but that is not compounding.

Debt compounds interest. Savings accounts compound interest. Investments do not. It is not the same thing!

Continuing with the philosophy, you "diversify" as a risk reduction strategy, so that if a certain sector of the market tanks, you don't have all of your money in that sector.

You "asset allocate" based on your time horizon (the number of years before you reach retirement age) and your "risk tolerance." The advisor does risk tolerance testing to see how much risk you are willing to take or can handle, based on your situation. In other words, how much of a drop in the value of your accounts can you handle without causing heart failure?

The goal is to get you in as risky of a position as you are comfortable taking, because "risk equals reward."

Over time, the closer you get to retirement age, the more your allocation should shift away from stocks and move towards bonds and other more secure investments. Some rules of thumb that exist say things like, "take one hundred minus your age, and that is the percentage of your assets that should be in stocks". Then, once you have reached the magic number that they told you was "your number," you retire and live on Social Security retirement income and the "safe withdrawal rate" from your retirement nest egg.

Also, at the time of retirement, you cancel your life insurance, and thereby "self-insure" going forward (more on this in Chapter 7).

Of course, all of this is extremely complex, so the planners subscribing to this theory say that you cannot do this on your own, and you need to pay someone to manage your money for you.

This sounds great to most people, as most people do not want to put in the additional time and effort that would be required to do the due diligence on investments before staking their future financial life on it.

The fees for asset management typically range from 1-3% per year of the total assets being managed. The less you have for them to manage, the more you will be charged. It's in your best interest to pay more, if you have less money to manage, right?

Actually, the truth is, clients don't usually receive proactive money management on amounts less than $1,000,000, and they receive no advice (other than generic brochures and allocation models) for money that is invested through qualified plans (401k's, 403b's, and so on).

The representatives who set up qualified plans for businesses are specifically told not to give any specific advice to any of the employees that are participating or considering participating. Pretty strange, right? It's just a "set the boat in the ocean and hope it goes the right direction" strategy.

Clients, on the other hand, do expect proactive money management. In other words, they do expect their money manager to call them and tell them that what they think the client should do to increase returns, avoid losses, etc., but that is not what happens.

To create an even greater impression that an advisor is going to proactively manager the client's investments, they have something new called "Account Aggregation."

Account aggregation, simply stated, is a way for an advisor and possibly even the client to login and see all of their investment accounts and their current real-time values. The impression this gives the client is that "if my advisor can see all of my investments all of the time, then he or she is going to watch them actively and let me know what I should do at all times." Does this happen? No. Does the client deserve the right to expect such proactive management if the advisor has real-time values at his/her fingertips every day? Yes.

The advice that is generally given to investors, whether stated this way or not, is this, "Just invest and then ignore whatever is happening in the market, up or down. Actually, just notice the upward movements and ignore the downward movements, because the downward movements are only real if you actually sell the security. Otherwise the downward movements are not 'realized' (real)."

Another way of saying it is, "buy and hold" for "the long haul." Unfortunately, "the long haul" really has no expiration.

Home > Retirement > Brett Arends's ROI

Brett Arends's ROI

Don't look at your 401(k)

Published: March 17, 2020 at 10:14 a.m. ET

By Brett Arends

Yes, it's down now — but that won't matter when you retire

Regarding investment management fees, Warren Buffet, who is a staunch supporter of stock market investing, has said that because of the high and diverse fees that investors pay, they will likely not receive anything close to the rates of return the stock market has provided in the past, which really kills the entire foundation of the Accumulation Theory-based plan.

Buffet said, "And that's where we are today: A record portion of the earnings that would go in their entirety to owners (owners of investments) – if they all just stayed in their rocking chairs – is now going to a swelling army of Helpers. Particularly expensive is the recent pandemic of profit arrangements under which Helpers receive large portions of the winnings when they are smart or lucky, and leave family members with all the losses – and large fixed fees to boot – when the Helpers are dumb or unlucky (or occasionally crooked)."

The "Helpers", he defines, are those in the securities business "helping" advise and manage people's money in the stock market. For the entire article, read the article *Cut Your Gains!* Fortune, March 20, 2006.

The "retirement nest egg" idea is the idea that a person can build a reservoir of money, and then live on that reservoir for the rest of his or her lifetime. The question has to be, how much is "enough" money in that reservoir?

It is really a silly and truly unanswerable question, without having access to a functioning crystal ball.

Many financial advisors try to answer this question for their clients by using mathematical calculations and lots of assumptions, such as inflation rates, rates of return during the withdrawal or income phase, "historical" stock market returns, future tax rates, clients' needs and desires, and so on.

The conversation usually starts with a question like this, "How much annual income do you need to live on in retirement?" Or maybe they will ask, "How much income would you like to live on in retirement?"

As nice as that question sounds, as much as it might be better than the financial advisor telling the client what he/she should want or need to live on, it is an extremely faulty foundation for the rest of the plan that will be built on top of the answer that is given to that question. Does the client know what things are going to cost? Does the client know what national or personal economic events are going to happen to them? Does the client know what their health situation is going to be like, and how much their care and lifestyle might cost in the future? What technology changes are going to happen in the next ten to twenty years?

Consider the fact that the internet didn't even exist more than 25 years ago. Consider the fact that the first iPhone didn't come out until 2007. Consider the fact that cars may cost as much twenty years from now as houses do today. There are too many things to consider for anyone to give an accurate answer to the question of how much money they will need to live on. Thus, attempts to predict the answer to that question and then build a plan on that answer are bound to fail.

Let's imagine we could predict the future. Let's imagine that a person who is making $100,000 in income today would either need or want that amount of income in retirement. How big would the reservoir ("nest egg") need to be in order to produce $100,000 per year of income?

We need to predict how long the person is going to live, and what interest rates are going to be at that time. Financial Planning has come up with something that makes that calculation easier. They call it the "safe withdrawal rate." The safe withdrawal rate is essentially the rate at which a person can take money out of their retirement portfolio without running out of money before they die.

Historically financial planning has used 4% as the safe withdrawal rate. More recent research on the topic, mainly by Dr. Wade Pfau, has proven that the 4% rate is too high based on today's persistent, extremely low-interest rate environment[1].

However, just for fun, let's use the 4% safe withdrawal rate. To know "your number" you need to divide the target annual income amount by the safe withdrawal rate.

$100,000 divided by .04 equals $2,500,000. Easy enough right? Makes sense, right?

This calculation is saying that a person would need $2,500,000 in her retirement investments (combined) in order to produce $100,000 per year without the chance of running out of money before she dies.

There are a few problems with this simple calculation. First, we failed to calculate inflation on the annual income amount. If we did that, at a 3% inflation rate, we would need an income of $180,611 twenty years from now in order to produce an income that feels like $100,000 does today.

Let's do the calculation again. $180,611 divided by .04 equals $4,515,275. That's a big difference in amount of money that is required! Let's see how much of this is riding on the safe withdrawal rate being 4%.

What if the safe withdrawal rate is actually 2% instead of 4%? How much money would the person have to have then?

---

[1] https://www.morningstar.com/articles/980620/wade-pfau-the-4-rule-is-no-longer-safe

Just $9,030,550. Super easy.

All I had to do is push a few different buttons on the calculator and voila!

The problem is that's not really how life and money works. If "our number" ends up being off by 40-60% of what we really need, we can't just push a button to solve the problem.

If interest rates end up being half of what we planned on, we can't just push a button to solve the problem.

If the investments underperform or have several years of significant losses, we can't just push a button to solve the problem.

Again, let's put aside reality and imagine that we *could* predict the future, that investments *could* compound at a predicted rate, and that the amount of money that we have come up with as a goal is real.

What amount of money would this person need to save (which is, by the way, the purpose of all of this crazy exercise) per year in order to reach their objective nest egg amount of money?

If a 45-year old, with 22 more years of work remaining, already has $200,000 saved in his retirement accounts to-date. We have to assume the rates of return the client will receive on his portfolio prior to retirement. We have to assume management fees as well.

First, let's talk about the stock market "historical rates of return." Many who love and promote the stock market say that the market has returned anywhere from 8-10% annual average rates of return. Honestly, I have no idea where they are coming up with that because in my working career of more than twenty years, that has not been the case, not even by a long shot.

On January 3, 2000, the S&P 500 closed at 1,441.47 point. On February 14, 2020 the S&P 500 closed at 3,380.16, which was the end of the longest bull run in the stock market's history.

I am not basing my argument on a period of time when the market has done poorly. What has been the return in the market since January 3, 2000? Has it been 8%? 10%?

Let's calculate it. Take the current value on February 14 (3,380.16) and subtract it from the initial value (1,441.47). That gives us 1,938.69. That is the total increase in the S&P 500 (which is broadly accepted as a measure of the stock market as a whole).

We then need to take that number and divide it into the initial value to find out the percentage increase over the time period. The answer is 134.49%. Sounds great, but that is not the annual return.

To get that number we need to divide total percent gain by the number of years (in this case we'll use 20 years, even though it has been slightly longer) and that will give us the (uncompounded) annual return. The answer is 6.73% per year.

To get the compounded rate of return, you have to use a compound interest calculator. Luckily, I have one. Put the initial value (1,441.47) in the Present Value of the calculator. Put the current value (3,380.16) in the Future Value of the calculator. Put 20 for the number of years, and then calculate.

The annual compounded interest rate for the S&P 500 over the past 20 years is 4.35%, which is nowhere near 8 or 10 percent.

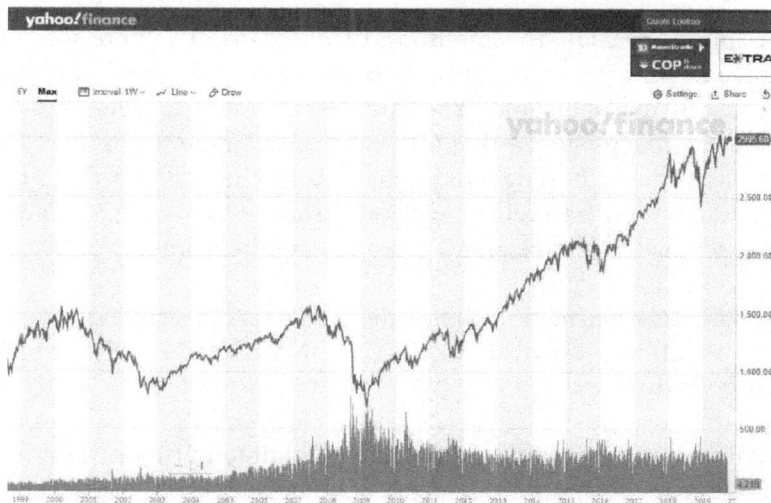

Let's say this client was a much luckier investor than most, and consistently outperformed the S&P 500 index over the next 22 years. Let's say he was able to earn an average of 6% per year. The funny thing is that most registered reps would say that is a "conservative" estimate. However, it is important to note that less than 5% of actively managed mutual funds outperform their benchmark index (Read *The Smartest Investment Book You'll Ever Read*, by Daniel R. Solin). There is a 95% chance that the funds an investor selects are going to underperform the index. Again, for this calculation, we will use the 6% annual rate of return.

Without any mutual fund or other management fees or taxes added to the calculation, the client would have to save/invest about *$84,000 per year* in order to reach the target nest egg amount.

That's a problem for someone that only makes $100,000 per year.

It is literally impossible. The person would have to save even more if we account for any taxes and any fees. That's really the bottom line with this strategy. It is actually impossible for someone to *save* their way to financial freedom.

Do people retire using this method? Yes, they do. Are there some that have been lucky enough to get in at exactly the right time and get out at exactly the right time? Yes. Are there some that are in high paying executive positions that are given stock grants and other forms of compensation or retirement packages that allows them to build enough wealth to retire very comfortably? Yes, but those are the exceptions to the rule and far from being the norm.

What really is the attraction to this method of wealth creation? I'll sum it up with two words, EASY and CONVENIENT. That's really what it boils down to.

How much knowledge and expertise are required in order to invest in the stock market, especially through mutual funds held inside a 401(k)? Zero. No knowledge is required.

How much additional effort is required from the investor? None.

They get hired and simply elect the percentage of their income they would like to contribute to the account. Wall Street has done an incredible job of making investing with them the easiest thing on earth.

How much money is required in order to invest? There is no requirement as far as I know. People can invest as little as $10 per month to get started.

Another thing that is attractive about following this strategy is that you have someone else to blame if things don't turn out well.

It's not your fault the market crashed.

It's not your fault your fund manager invested in underperforming or losing businesses.

It's not your fault your fund manager lied to you or charged you more money in fees than they said in the prospectus.

It's not your fault your employer stopped matching your contributions to your account.

This mentality is not a trait of successful investors or successful people in general. Successful people, in any arena, do not look for ways to blame others for their problems or downfall. They want to be held accountable. They want the buck to stop with them. Accountability is a principle that leads to success. Lack of accountability *always* leads to failure.

Chapter 4: Saving and Investing Are Not the Same Thing

Wall Street, which is the major beneficiary of promoting the Accumulation Method, has done an amazing job of marketing and promoting the theory. They understand the power of words.

For example, during the period of the Great Depression in the United States, investing in the stock market was actually called "speculating." Over time they changed the word to "investing." Investing sounds more sophisticated, and less like gambling.

More recently, financial institutions have become wise and they have changed the word to "saving."

Are speculating, investing, and saving the same thing? Of course they aren't!

Speculating sounds risky, like pulling the handle on a slot machine or something you do at a horse race.

Investing sounds like a lot of additional work, and something that requires specialized knowledge.

Saving sounds like something very safe, something you really do not need to know a lot about in order to do it, and something everyone should do.

Save = Safe

Knowing this, doesn't it make sense that financial planners and financial instutions call retirement investment accounts "retirement savings" and 529 plans "college savings plans?"

People are being taught that they "should save for retirement." This is intentional. It is, in fact, designed to deceive customers, who otherwise might not want to put their money at risk, into investing in the market.

The word "invest" means "to cover completely." Cover completely, to me, means that you take the time to do the research and become educated as much as possible before putting your money into something.

At a minimum, you would think that if a person were going to invest in some sort of investment, they would want to know who is managing their money in that investment.

With more than twenty years of experience doing financial planning with hundreds of individuals who have had money invested in mutual funds, not one could tell me the name of the manager of any of the funds where they had money invested.

Wall Street is not encouraging people to invest. Wall Street is encouraging people to gamble.

Gamble means "to play games of chance for money," "take risky action in the hope of a desired result."

Synonyms of Gamble are: bet, wager, speculation. How do you convince a ton of people to put their hard-earned money at risk who otherwise would not?

First, make it easy and convenient.

Second, make it sound safe.

How effective has the marketing been from Wall Street? In 1929 only ten percent of Americans had money in the stock market. Today, about 52% of Americans own stock in the stock market (Financial Samurai, What Percent of Americans Own Stocks?).

Imagine the impact of a Great Depression today! If you have not already seen it, I encourage you to watch The Retirement Gamble, a PBS Frontline Documentary. This documentary exposes the issues of hidden and undisclosed investment management fees, and the truth that Wall Street does in fact encourage gambling, not investing, and they disguise it with the word "save" or "savings."

Chapter 5: Risk Equals Reward

Financial planners teach that risk equals reward. This is what I call a half-truth. Yes, if a person ever wants to create wealth, they will need to do something other than put their money in guaranteed products and accounts. Anything other than guaranteed products and accounts does have risk of loss of principal associated with it.

All investments have the potential to lose money. None are excluded. That is what classifies something as an investment. When I hear people say that life insurance is a bad investment, for example, I say, "You're right! It's a bad investment because it's not actually an investment at all." It's like saying that a hammer is a bad screwdriver. They are not in the same category, except when you're talking about all tools.

Life insurance is a financial tool, and so is an investment. However, they aren't the same kind of tool and they don't perform the same function. It's a bad comparison at best.

Life insurance is a guaranteed product (at least whole life insurance is) and no investment is.

Life insurance creates guaranteed liquid cash. Investments do not.

Life insurance has a death benefit, investments do not.

Life insurance provides disability protection and long-term care-type benefits. Investments do not.

Again, it's just a bad comparison. I'm not saying one is better than the other. That is like saying a hammer is better or more important than a screwdriver. I am saying that it's not right, nor is it helpful to compare the two.

When financial advisors say, "risk equals reward," what they are saying is that the more risk you are willing to take, the greater the potential reward. If this were true, then the very best investments would be in the casinos in Las Vegas or the state lotteries. There's an extremely high amount of risk of loss, so the potential gain must also be very high.

However, gambling almost always leads to loss, especially in the long-term. And what is downplayed even more is any sense of control in the situation. Investing based on this idea is simply throwing money in the game of chance, and the more you are willing to lose, the greater your return over time. What this idea promotes is that in order to ever achieve returns that are sufficient to grow your retirement nest egg, you have to be willing to take high levels of risk with your money. This is false.

The house always wins.

What is risk really associated with when it comes to investing, and how does a client minimize it? Let's say that I'm thinking about starting a dental practice. I'm not a dentist. I have no experience in dental practice (other than being treated myself). I've never hired or worked with dental technicians, receptionists, or hygienists. I have no idea what to look for. I have no idea what equipment will be needed, other than the tools I've seen at my dental appointments (I don't even know what most of them are called).

Would investing in a dental practice for me be a risky investment? Of course! How likely would I lose money in the investment? Probably very likely. I would not practice the dentistry myself, as I know that would be illegal, but I could hire someone else. It's probably a bad investment for me.

What if I have a client who is a good dentist? What about the risk for him? Let's say he has been in dentistry for several years, working for another dentist, observing not only how the dentist performs dentistry, but also learning how to run the practice (the hiring and training of staff, dealing with the financial side, dealing with insurance companies, etc.).

Let's say this dentist client has an opportunity to start his own practice or buy out an existing practice. In comparison to me, what is the risk for loss of investment for the dentist client? Probably significantly lower. What is the difference? KNOWLEDGE and experience.

It could be the same exact investment opportunity that we are talking about. Risk is not something that is innate to the investment itself as much as it is associated with the level of knowledge and experience of the person investing, the investor.

We have heard the phrase, "knowledge is power." Well, knowledge reduces risk. The more you know about something, the less risky it is to you. This is why investing is very individualized. Investing is more about *becoming something* than it is about where you put your money.

It is the client's responsibility to decide what he/she is going to become an expert in, not the advisor's. It is the client's responsibility to decide where they are going to invest. They should invest where they are willing to become experts.

The assets under management world wants you to believe that diversification is what reduces risk. That's not entirely true. In fact, diversification, while it may reduce your changes of losing all of your money in one place, does in fact expose you to a greater chance of losing money somewhere.

If a portfolio was perfectly diversified, wouldn't the gains from some investments be perfectly offset by the losses of other investments at the same time?

Have you ever heard the phrase "Jack of all trades and master of none?"

I like to say it this way, "Isn't it better to have an inch-wide, mile-deep level of expertise than a mile-wide inch-deep level of expertise?" Specialization is what really creates wealth, not diversification.

Specialization is having an inch-wide mile-deep level of knowledge. Who earns more money, a general practice doctor or a specialist such as a neurosurgeon? Knowledge is what reduces risk and creates the potential for much higher rates of return. The great financial book *Think and Grow Rich* by Napoleon Hill states that one of the key factors of becoming rich is "Specialized Knowledge." That's what we are talking about here. General knowledge is not what creates wealth.

Another risk-factor is CONTROL. If you invest in something that you have no control of and no expertise in, what direction does your risk of loss of principal go? It goes up.

If you invest in something where you have a large amount of control and a high level of expertise, what direction does your risk of loss of principal go? It goes down.

Would financial institutions invest their money into things where they give up control and have little or no expertise? Of course not.

No one cares about your money more than you do, and that's because only you know the amount of work you put forth in order to receive that money. Giving up control increases risk. One of the major objectives of financial institutions is for you to give up control so that they can have use of your money for long periods of time.

They do this through financial tools like 401(k)'s, IRA's, SEP's, SIMPLE's, 529 plans, and so on. Those types of accounts are designed prevent your access to your money for long periods of time without being subject to penalties and taxes. You can only access the money for specific purposes and at the specific times that they have laid out. Interestingly, most clients that I have worked with are unclear on when they can access their money without paying a penalty.

Those financial tools are what I call "single-use" products and strategies. They are designed for one purpose, and if they are used for any other purpose you get penalized.

For example, a 529 plan gives the owner of the account some perceived benefits of state income-tax deductible contributions (but only if you live in the state where the plan is being managed) and tax-free distributions for qualifying education-related expenses.

What happens if something comes up and you need the money to pay for medical expenses for yourself or a family member? If you use the money for that purpose, you are penalized and taxed. 529 plans have a singleuse and a single purpose. That is one-way financial institutions promote what benefits them the most.

If control is what financial institutions and highly successful investors want with their money, and they do what they can to avoid giving it up, shouldn't you try to do the same?

Chapter 6: Average Rates of Return

One thing that is heavily marketed and causes people to make major mistakes is basing investment decisions on "average" and projected rates of return, instead of truly researching and investigating an investment.

Researching an investment is much more than calculating the projected rates of return and the impact that it will have on your net worth. Marketing pieces produced by the funds themselves or favorably biased institutions that focus almost solely on historical average rates of return for a fund, for example, is not research. In fact, the funds themselves state that "past rates of return are no indication/guarantee of future results."

Investing this way could be compared to driving a car while only looking through the rearview mirror. I call this method of investing, "chasing returns." People that chase returns will almost certainly lose their money at some point.

Statistically, averages mean almost nothing by themselves. In fact, averages can be very deceiving. Let me ask you, is it possible to average a positive rate of return and still lose money? Sounds impossible, right?

I'm going to prove it to you. Let's say you invested $100 into something that gave you a 100% return in the first year. What is your total balance by the end of the first year? $200.

Let's say you have a loss of 60% the next year. What is your balance? $80.

What was the average rate of return? To get the average you have to take the sum of each annual return and divide it by the total number of years. Add 100% + negative 60% and you get 40%. Divide that by two and you get 20% per year. That is POSITIVE 20% per year.

Is it true that the average rate of return is positive 20% per year? Yes. Is it deceiving? Yes. It is deceiving because if someone told you they averaged a positive 20% return per year, would you assume they lost money? Of course not.

What matters in this scenario is that you lost money overall. What doesn't matter is the average rate of return.

Table 2 provides an example of how an investment averaging 7.5% return can actually outperform an investment averaging 10.5% return. Using mathematical formulas alone, such as average rates of return, as the sole means of evaluating financial decisions can be a financially devastating mistake, because what really happens is usually very different from the averages.

Table 2 – Averages Mean Nothing

Annual Investment	Account 1 Annual Returns	7.5% Account balance	Account 2 Annual Returns	10.5% Account balance
$10,000.00	10.00%	$11,000.00	12.00%	$11,200.00
$10,000.00	-1.00%	$20,790.00	-15.00%	$18,020.00
$10,000.00	5.00%	$32,329.50	25.00%	$35,025.00
$10,000.00	-3.00%	$41,059.62	45.00%	$65,286.25
$10,000.00	12.00%	$57,186.77	28.00%	$96,366.40
$10,000.00	9.00%	$73,233.58	-12.00%	$93,602.43
$10,000.00	1.00%	$84,065.91	15.00%	$119,142.80
$10,000.00	15.00%	$108,175.80	6.00%	$136,891.36
$10,000.00	11.00%	$131,175.14	14.00%	$167,456.16
$10,000.00	-2.00%	$138,351.64	-18.00%	$145,514.05
$10,000.00	12.00%	$166,153.83	15.00%	$178,841.15
$10,000.00	8.00%	$190,246.14	30.00%	$245,493.50
$10,000.00	16.00%	$232,285.52	12.00%	$286,152.72
$10,000.00	12.00%	$271,359.78	-10.00%	$266,537.45
Totals	7.50% Average	$271,359.78 ending balance	10.50% Average	$266,537.45 ending balance

Although it can be helpful to use math to evaluate or test a strategy, basing financial decisions on solid economic principles provides us with a proper framework upon which to achieve financial success.

People should never base an investment decision primarily on projected rates of return. Projected rates of return can be deceiving, and they oftentimes encourage people to invest in things where they give up control and expertise.

Projected rates of return cause people to become starry-eyed and to look past and ignore the risks that are associated with investments and forego doing their due diligence before investing.

Investing based mainly on projected rates of return is a recipe for loss.

Chapter 7: Self-Insure – The Road to Fear of Use of Assets

Another major tenet of the Accumulation Theory is the idea of self-Insuring in retirement. What does that mean? When you retire you cancel your life insurance because at that point in time, "you don't need life insurance anymore."

With self-insurance, instead of using life insurance to provide for your spouse if he/she happens to outlive you, you use your assets to insure one another. How does that work? More importantly, is that the best approach to insuring?

The accumulation theorists believe that the only reason a person should own life insurance is to insure his/her income to a family PRIOR TO reaching the goal of retirement. Once a person retires, the purpose of life insurance does not exist anymore because the person is no longer going to be working for income. Therefore, they do not "need" life insurance anymore.

What are the effects of following this idea?

Would it surprise you to find out that financial institutions actually benefit the most from this strategy?

Imagine you own a home and you make your final mortgage payment on it. You now own the home free and clear. Prior to this time, the mortgage lender forced you to buy homeowners insurance on your house.

The type of homeowners insurance they required was "full replacement cost" coverage. This means that they required that you had the type of insurance coverage that would completely rebuild your house if necessary, based on damage from any of the hazards that are covered in the policy. In fact, there is even wiggle room in most homeowners policies that will provide an additional level of coverage up to 125% of the stated dwelling coverage amount (in case costs for materials and labor spiked suddenly).

The mortgage company is not concerned about rebuilding just the house you need (the minimal amount of building you need to live in), they want full replacement of the actual house, whether you or they need it or not. The house is an asset, and they want to protect the full value.

In this example, you now own your house outright. At this point you aren't required by anyone to maintain homeowners insurance anymore. Are you going to cancel your homeowners insurance?

My guess is that you would say "no." You would likely want to keep your homeowners insurance. Why? Because now you have more to lose if something does happen to the house.

What if you had enough money in the bank to rebuild your house? The cash in the bank would be your insurance on your house. Would that be a good idea? Why or why not? I ask clients these exact questions, and I have never had a client say that they would like that idea. They always say that they would prefer to carry homeowners insurance.

When I ask the client why they would want homeowners insurance instead of using their money to self-insure in the bank, they say, "because if I have homeowners insurance, then I can do whatever else I want with the money in the bank." EXACTLY.

What is the effect of self-insuring? It locks up your money or assets so that they cannot be used for anything else. Is that what you want to do with your money when you retire?

Have you ever wondered why the number one concern for retirees is that they will run out of money sometime before they die? Do you think that self-insuring has at least a small part to play in the cause for that fear or concern? If the result of self-insuring is that you feel you cannot use/spend/enjoy your assets, can you imagine anything else a financial institution would want more than this? If they can convince you to give them your money and never touch it again, that is their objective.

Part III: The Velocity of Money

Chapter 8: The Velocity of Money

The Velocity of Money is an economic principle. It is not a product or a specific strategy. It isn't even specific to personal financial planning.

Investopedia (Reviewed by James Chen updated 09/10/2019) defines velocity of money as "a measurement of the rate at which money moves from one entity to another. It also refers to how much a unit of currency is used in a given period of time. The velocity of money is important for measuring the rate at which money in circulation is being used for purchasing goods and services. It is used to help economists and investors gauge the health and vitality of an economy."

To summarize in my own words, velocity of money is a measure of the *number of uses of the same dollar* in a plan over a period of time. It has a direct impact on the financial health and well-being of an individual's personal economy.

The more money moves from one person to another in a national economy the healthier the economy becomes, and the richer those living in it become. In other words, the greater the velocity, the more wealth is created.

The opposite is also true. The less movement of money, the more money stagnates, the poorer an economy becomes and those living in it.

It is clear that the greater the velocity of money the better for an economy and for businesses, but what about individuals? That is where traditional financial planning, which follows the accumulation method, and I depart from one another.

Traditional financial planning almost entirely ignores economic principles and instead uses mathematics to support their ideas and strategies. Traditional planning, for instance, does not measure opportunity costs, which is something business and national economists always strive to measure and minimize. Efficiency and effectiveness are the goal of businesses, whereas rate of return is the goal of traditional planning.

How do we implement economic principles into financial planning for individuals? Many are doing it already, even if they don't know that it's called velocity of money. In fact, many are attracted to the idea of it, again, even though they don't know what it's called.

Here is an example. In the United States, most people want to own a home instead of renting a home or apartment for the rest of their lives. Why is that? When I ask clients, they say, "Because I don't like throwing money away." Most people view renting as "throwing money away."

When I ask them why they want to own a house, they say, "Because I build equity." What is the benefit of building equity? Clients say, "It is money that I will get back some day."

Buying a house is a way to increase velocity, or the number of uses of my money during my life. Again, remember what financial institutions want us to do. They want us to participate in one-use products and strategies. Renting is a one-use strategy. You pay your rent, you get a roof over your head for a period of time, and you never see that money again.

Rent   or   **Buy**

One-Use Vehicle   Multi-Use Vehicle

If you put money in a 529 plan, you use that to pay for your children's education, and you will never see that money again. One use. I am not saying it is worth it or not worth it. I am saying the money is not coming back to be used again.

What if there were ways to increase the velocity of your money in more areas of your life than just buying a home? Would you want to know about it? Especially if it is a principle that has proven to create more wealth for entire nations and peoples over the history of the earth?

I am going to teach you how. It is what financial institutions do, but the opposite of what they teach. It is what the wealthiest people in the world do to create their wealth and financial independence.

You can, and I will explain how. The next five chapters will each introduce a principle of personal finance that will increase the velocity of money in your own life. If you follow the principles of personal finance that successful financial institutions and highly successful individuals use to create, utilize, and protect wealth, you will achieve the same result.

Chapter 9: Principle #1 – Save 15% or More

The first principle is where the velocity of money method begins. No one will create wealth without saving money, unless the wealth is inherited. Saving appears to be one of the most difficult things for people to do. Based on a recent article on CNBC the average American household has only $8,863 in savings (Source: 2016 Survey of Consumer Finances). That almost paints a better picture than what is really happening.

About 30% of households have less than $1,000 in savings. In my own experience as a financial planner, what I commonly see is much less than one month of household income in liquid savings, large amounts of credit card and other debts (student loan debt is at epidemic proportions) at annual compounding interest rates of 8-28%, and the only systematic saving that is happening is going into their retirement plans.

As a side note, the average amount of money going into savings decreases when the economy and stock market improve. Why is that? Maybe it has something to do with the accumulation theory, which has told them how much money they need in the future.

If their accounts are doing better than expected, they do not need to save as much. If the average rates of return are higher, they don't need to save as much. Right? Wrong. That is why saving is a principle, not something that is determined by predictions or rates of return.

Why is saving so hard, and why is it so important? The desire to consume is huge. We are constantly being marketed to buy this or buy that. No matter how much money you make, you can spend it.

It is shocking to see former popular singers, actors, and athletes who made millions upon millions of dollars completely broke just a few years after they ended their careers. We can learn from them.

It is shocking to see how people that win the lottery so often end up being worse off financially than they were before they won the lottery. We can learn from them.

There are a few secrets to becoming successful at saving money. The first one is that the "why" for saving has to be greater than the "why not". Saving is all about the future. It is about something that is less tangible than the things you could spend the money on right now (especially with Amazon Prime).

Delayed gratification is what is required for saving to work. The only way delayed gratification works is if the reason you are delaying is bigger, or more important, than the reason you would not delay. In other words, your future freedom from having to work for money has to be more important, and just as clear, as the reason you want to buy that nice new vehicle, or that nicer bigger house. In fact, if your reason for saving is not clear, it cannot be very motivating, and you will not stick to it.

In psychology there are two types of motivators or reinforcers: positive reinforcers and negative reinforcers. A positive reinforcer is something that motivates you strive for a good result. A negative reinforcer is something that motivates you to avoid a bad result.

For example, let's talk about the speed limit. A positive reinforcer for obeying the speed limit might be so that you make it safely home to your family. A negative reinforcer for this situation might be to avoid paying a fine on a speeding ticket. Either can be sufficiently motivating.

The same can be applied to motivations for saving. For someone, the desire to be financially free, to be able to set their own daily schedule, to donate to whatever charitable cause they want, in the amount they want, and so on, might be their positive reinforcer. They may also have some negative reinforcers, which might include not ending up financially dependent like their parents, not paying interest on credit cards their whole lives, or not having to "work for the man" their entire lives. Whatever the motivations are, positive and/or negative, each person has to define for themselves, make them clear, and not lose sight of them.

The question your clients need to be able to answer, and that you cannot give them, is *why* they are saving. What does their future look like if they do save? Are they going to travel? Where are they going to travel? Are they going to donate more to charities? If they were financially free, what would they like to do? They need to talk about this and come up with their own reasons for why and they need to make those as clear as possible.

Several years ago, I lost a large amount of weight. The key to my weight loss was that I was very clear about *why* I wanted to lose weight and the benefits that I thought I would receive by losing it. It was motivating enough to me that I could say no to bad food choices, as tempting as they were. My goal was more important to me than the temporary satisfaction I would receive by compromising in the moment.

This principle applies to long-term savings as well. The why has to be greater than the why not.

Another reason why savings is so difficult for most people is because they don't have a good system for saving. For many people, outside of the amount they save in their employer retirement plan, they save only after they have spent their money on whatever else they have wanted to buy, and all of the bills are paid.

This bottom-of-the-totem pole strategy only works well for extremely frugal individuals, and the fact that they save money is more oftentimes related to a fear of money than something that they are being proactive about. I am not saying there is anything wrong with frugality, as I believe that is an important aspect of wealth creation. "Waste not, want not."

Saving should be systematic and automatic. Automatic meaning that it is something that happens without you having to think about it every time. Systematic meaning that you have a way of doing it that makes it a priority and something that you are proactively doing, versus passively doing.

The strategy I recommend to clients regarding their savings works out very well for people that are paid by direct deposit. In most situations, the client can go to their employer or HR and request that a portion of their gross pay be deposited in a separate account, one that is designated for the sole purpose of long-term wealth building. This makes their saving happen first, every time they are paid, and instead of the money going into the account that is used to pay all of the bills and living expenses, it goes into an account that has a longer-term purpose. It simply happens every time the person is paid.

My recommendation is that clients save at least 15% of their income. In the movie *Up*, a Disney/Pixar animation that came out in 2009, it portrays a couple that is in love and gets married. During the first few minutes of the film, it shows them growing older together and experiencing life.

They have this overarching goal in their lives that they start saving money for. Over time it shows them putting money into the jar, but every time the jar starts to get full, they have to spend it all for some unexpected life event. The story ends tragically when the wife passes away due to illness. I don't think I've ever seen a cartoon before that made me cry, but this one did.

For those that save, but don't save enough of their income, they will end up depleting their savings every time some major or minor life event happens. How do you save enough for unexpected life events as well as the achievement of your future financial freedom?

For those that don't save at all, every time life events happen they borrow money. This puts them on the side of paying interest their entire lives instead of making interest.

The reality is, I don't know if saving 15% is enough. There is no guarantee that it is. Every life is unique and unique sets of circumstances happen to them. What I do know is, the more they save, the better off they will be, the more prepared they will be, the less likely they will go into debt for things.

I could give you more "concrete" reasons to save, such as future medical costs, planned obsolescence, technology changes, changes to fads and trends, and lifestyle changes, but the truth is, I cannot predict, nor can anyone else, what those things are going to cost exactly.

Saving 15% of your income means that you get used to living on 85% of your income. I believe that is something most people can do, especially if they do it from the beginning.

Work and Earn

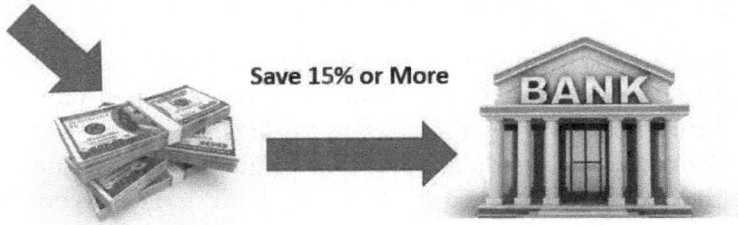

Save 15% or More

BANK

Chapter 10: Principle #2 – Maximum Protection

There are only three or four possible reasons why people don't have maximum insurance protection.

First, they might not know about it. This is probably true for almost 100% of your clients.

Second, most advisors don't offer it to their clients. Whose choice should it be? Yours as the advisor or your clients'?

Third, the perception of cost. I say perception because most clients really don't know what it would cost to obtain the maximum protection. In their minds, whatever it is, it must be a lot! The thought prevents them from finding out. In conjunction with this, they have been trained by the assets-under-management industry to think of insurance as something that is detrimental to wealth creation.

Fourth, they don't really think they are vulnerable. Bad things only happen to other people, not me. I'll address each of these reasons.

Can you buy too much insurance? Can you be "insurance poor"? Can you protect your finances too much? I guess it's possible in some areas to over-protect, but I have yet to see that in all the years I've done planning.

Generally, the idea of being "insurance poor" is an excuse for a lack of financial education and a lack dedication to saving. The reason someone fails in their saving and investing usually has nothing to do with their level of insurance coverage. In fact, what I have found is that the people with the most insurance usually also have the most wealth. So, if having protection was an impingement to wealth creation, then wouldn't the wealthiest people have the least amount of insurance and protection?

How do we figure out what our maximum protection is? Let me begin to answer this by asking a few questions.

If you knew you were going to die tomorrow, but you could get more life insurance today, what amount of life insurance would you purchase?

If you knew you were going to be involved in a serious auto accident tomorrow where you severely injure or kill someone, how much liability protection would you want?

If you knew you were going to become too sick or injured to do your job, but you could get disability insurance today, what kind of protection would you want?

We could go on with different questions regarding each area of protection that a person can use insurance or legal documents to protect against. The answers clients give to each of these questions has never once been, "well, let me calculate the amount my family would need, or let me calculate how much disability insurance my family would need." Those are never the response.

The response is always, "as much as I could get," or "the best that I could get." The only time that people want less than their maximum is when they don't think something is going to happen to them. When a person knows and understands that the event can happen to them, and without proper protection they could lose everything financially, cost becomes almost irrelevant.

Some people really feel like nothing is ever going to happen to them. If they feel this way, there may not be much you can do to help them. As an advisor, the sooner you can find out about this feeling, the better. In the relationship between a planner and a client, both have the power to end the relationship. Sometimes it's necessary to fire a client.

In those situations where the client feels invincible, they probably just need to experience life for a little while and eventually they will discover that they are not invincible. No one plans on becoming sick, disabled, getting sued, dying early, or having a serious accident, but it still happens every day to many people, people that we all know. That is why financial planning is important. It is not to predict anything. It is to protect and be in the best position possible for whatever life throws your way.

Many people have what I call "pretend protection." They have minimal amounts of coverage, or "a good amount of coverage," on everything simply to appease their spouse (or their own conscience). They may have certain levels of coverage because they thought "it's the right thing to do," "the adult thing to do," or because "it's required by law."

I always think it's important to ask clients why they have the coverage they have. How did they come to choose the amount of coverage they have? Most of the time the answers are, "that's just what I've always had," "it's what the agent sold me," "I felt like it was a good amount," or "it would pay off my mortgage and a little bit more." As they express why they have the amount of coverage they have in each area of protection, I believe most come to realize that their reasoning is a sandy foundation.

Let's look at another aspect of protection, the insurance side. Is it really possible to "over-insure?" If I own a house and the cost to replace the house is $300,000, can I purchase dwelling coverage for a $1,000,000 house?

If I make $100,000 per year in income, and I am 45 years old, can I purchase $10,000,000 of life insurance and a disability policy with a $30,000 per month benefit?

The answer to both questions is no.

Most clients do not know this, because no one tells them about it. Insurance companies have underwriting limits. Those limits are based on the real assets they are insuring. Insurance companies indemnify for an insured loss. They never make it so that the insurance would put a person in a better financial position if the event they are insuring against actually happens. This would be counterproductive. People would purposely allow their houses to burn down, they would purposely allow themselves to become sick or injured, and some might even try to die early.

The insurance company will never purposely make it profitable to you to make a claim. Now that we have brought that up, can a person "over-insure?" The answer is no. They cannot because the insurance companies will not issue a policy that would allow that to happen.

Now maybe what people mean when they say, "over-insure" is that they feel that if they buy their maximum protection, that they will have less money to spend, or to invest. While I suppose that may be a possibility, I have yet to witness that in anyone's financial situation. Whether the person has more or less to spend or invest generally has much more to do with other lifestyle decisions than the amount insurance they carry.

My question is what is the priority? In most cases it is clear that the priority is to spend and consume as much of their income as possible right now. The priority is to "keep up with the Joneses."

For those financial planners who are interested in minimizing insurance and protection so that their clients can invest more, how much of a difference does that difference in premium really make per year? Do your clients really "save the difference?"? Or is the recommendation to lower insurance coverage more out of an interest to have as much money in assets under management as possible? If the event your clients are protecting against actually happens, are you willing to make up the difference to them between the coverage you recommended and the maximum they could have had? In my opinion, you should be. Sacrificing protection for the sake of a slight increase in future investment values should never be the objective of the financial planner. The choice for maximum protection should never be the advisor's. It should be the client's choice.

I have never seen a case where someone had so much money going towards protection that they could not save anything. What I have seen is people spending so much money on lifestyle that they cannot save and do not have the type of protection they would really want if the events they are insuring against actually happen. Instead of addressing the real financial problem in a client's situation, which is usually spending habits, the easier target for a financial advisor is insurance. That "necessary evil" as they often call it. It's easier for the planner to lower insurance and redirect money to investments than it is to encourage a client to do a better job of tracking their income and expenses.

What most clients (and advisors) choose to sacrifice is not lifestyle and what most advisors choose to sacrifice isn't "investing." They choose to sacrifice their protection and savings. Why? They (the clients and advisors) must not believe something is really going to happen to them, so, they buy a little protection and hope for the best. That's what I call pretend protection.

Many times, if you do offer maximum protection, your clients have been trained to respond with, "Do I really need that amount of coverage?" Unless you have a functioning crystal ball, you do not know the answer to that question, and neither do they. My question is, "If your house burns down to the ground and everything in it, what would you like rebuilt and replaced?" Most likely, the client will say, "I want everything replaced and rebuilt". My follow up to that is, "Even if you don't need it? Even if you really don't need that big or nice of a house? Even if you don't need that much or nice of furniture?" To which they will say, "Yes, I would want it all replaced." Another great question to ask is, "Mr & Mrs Client, you make X amount of money each year. Do you make a little more money than you absolutely need?" In most cases, the answer is "yes". I follow that with, "Is there ever a time when you will get paid more than what you absolutely need, and you'll send the money back?" The answer is always, "No!" "So, if we are insuring your income, or your house, or any other asset of yours, it's really not about what you need is it?" Then I state, "It's about replacing what you have isn't it?" They usually get the point that I am making.

Insurance and protection are not about need. Protection and insurance are about what people want. It is about replacing a real asset that the client chose to have in their life, whether that is their income or their property.

The next issue clients will have in their minds is cost. What does it cost to have maximum protection? This is definitely something that clients are going to be concerned about.

The first thing that I believe is important to remember, as an advisor, is that the client really does not know what it costs. They probably imagine it is really expensive, something they cannot afford. But the truth is, they don't know what the cost is, because no advisor they've met with before has ever let them know what their maximum is. It is important to remember that going into it.

For example, does a client who has never been offered a personal liability umbrella policy know what a $1,000,000 policy costs? Of course not. In most cases, they didn't even know it existed! When they find out that the annual premium for an umbrella policy is usually around $200-$300, they are amazed at how cheap it is. When they realize that this is a way for them to multiply the level of their liability protection without multiplying their premium, they usually want it.

For another example, if the client has $100,000 per person bodily injury liability on their auto insurance, to raise it to $250,000 they may think that their premium is going to more than double. However, it is going to be a tiny increase in premium in most cases. In many cases you can encourage your clients to get quotes from other insurance carriers and potentially make all of the recommended changes to their auto, homeowners, and liability, without any additional premium. This has happened more times than I can count for clients in my own practice.

What I have found is that people find a way to pay for things that they feel are important to them. If it is not important to them, they will find a lot of excuses as to why they can't afford it.

It's important to realize that you have a big influence on what your clients feel is important. If you do not treat protection as important and as the foundation of a strong financial plan, there is a good chance they will not either. From a professional liability standpoint, wouldn't it better to express the importance of protection? In psychology terms, this is called "projecting." Be careful not to project a lack of importance in the protection area of a person's finances. Instead, purposely project a high level of importance, and you may be surprised to find that your clients also see it that way. Do not let your obstacles become their obstacles to maximizing their protection.

My advice to you, as the advisor, is that you do not make any decisions for your clients. Give your clients the power to make decisions for themselves. Help them understand what their options are, why they should consider getting their maximum protection, and how they can accomplish it, and then let them decide what they are going to do.

I believe advisors have an obligation to their clients to let them know the level of protection they could have, instead of only telling them about the things they think their clients are going to be willing to buy. The approach is simple and doesn't require any type of "power phrase," memorized speech, or canned PowerPoint presentation.

Only tell them what
I think they'll buy.

Tell them what
they could have.

What kind of protection would the person want if the event they are protecting against (death, lawsuit, fire, disability, etc.) actually happens? That is the level of protection you should be telling your clients about. Forget whether or not you think they are going to be willing to buy it or not. Maybe they can't, or maybe they won't. That is not your choice.

You are never going to be sued for giving your clients the option. However, you may be sued, and you will definitely regret not giving your clients the option. If the client has less than maximum because they chose such, that is completely different from the client not having their maximum because you did not tell them about it.

What about inserting your opinion into the equation? If you had a serious illness or injury and went to the doctor, would you want a doctor that sat down and gave you a bunch of different options for treating the issue and said, "it doesn't matter to me which one you choose. We'll just do whatever you want," or would you prefer to have a doctor that is totally biased based on his experience and expertise and tells you which option he feels will solve the problem most effectively?

There is a lot of silly conversation and marketing out there within the financial services industry trying to encourage people to go to a fee-based advisor because they are "unbiased." This gives the client the impression that they could choose an advisor that will simply explain their options and has no vested interest in which option they choose because they don't get paid a commission. This is bologna. Everyone has an opinion on what works and what does not work. Clients want to know what your opinion is. Would you really want to go to a doctor who really does not have a strong opinion on what would be best for you?

One final point I want to make about this principle is that you should be careful not to get "into the weeds" regarding the specific product (i.e. type of life insurance) when discussing this principle. At this point, we are not talking about the type of product. We are talking about the level of coverage and the quality of protection. When a person dies, the surviving beneficiary does not care what type of life insurance it was, whether it was group term, individual term, universal life, or whole life. What they do care about is the amount of benefit that is paid out. In this philosophy, the type of life insurance is less important than the amount of coverage.

Stick to the principle.

Recently I asked a long-time client of mine if he would be willing to share his story related to the importance of life insurance, and specifically the importance of life insurance on a non-income earning spouse.

In his case, he had no life insurance on his first wife prior to me meeting with them. His first wife was a non-income earning spouse. In my career, she was also the first client of mine to pass away. A young mother with two small children. Most of the financial planning world, which focuses on selling insurance based on "needs," would either eliminate or diminish the importance of life insurance on a non-income earning spouse.

However, because I teach principles instead of predictions, I always let my clients know what they can have for protection, encourage them to get their maximum, and let them make the decision on whether or not they believe it's important enough to get. Here is the story my client gave permission for me to share (names have been changed for privacy):

> *"Sorry to take so long to get back to you. To say the least, it's been an interesting few weeks since you wrote and asked me to share my thoughts on life insurance. I find it interesting that you would reach out to me about life insurance for spouses that don't work or aren't the primary breadwinner in a family.*

> *"My current wife Katie, age 33, just had surgery on Tuesday for a double mastectomy due to a breast cancer diagnosis. She has no family history of the disease and no genetic markers, yet suddenly here we are wrapped up in a world of breast surgeons, plastic surgeons and oncologists. Here we are in a place where the thought to get more life insurance a year ago, six months ago, at the start of the year was placed on the back burner, because she's only 33 right? And she's been working on getting in better shape which means a better rate right? Now here we are in quite literally a battle for her life with no option but the current life insurance we have, which we are incredibly grateful to have in the event of the worst happening, but is woefully less than we should have.*

"This of course comes just short of 10 years from the day my first wife Mary, age 31, passed away unexpectedly while lying in bed next to me. I'm not sure I can express how comforting it was to know that with all of the grief that comes with losing a spouse, and trying to explain to children too young to fully comprehend why their mother wasn't coming home again; that I could focus on those things and not have to worry about funeral expenses (almost $15,000), house payments, taking time off work, and so many other things because of a life insurance policy we decided to get several years before. As the person that goes to work, you always assume that if something catastrophic is going to happen, it's going to happen to you; but the catastrophe that is every bit as real is losing the person staying home, taking care of the kids, house, pets, errands and every other thing while you're out working for the means to provide those things. I can't imagine how difficult it must be for those people who lose their spouse and are forced to go back to work much sooner than should because they didn't make a plan to provide life insurance for their spouse.

"I can't state emphatically enough how important it is to have life insurance on both parents, and children as well if finances allow. Start when you're young, invest in whole life if you can find any way at all to afford it, even if you have to stretch things a little at first, because you'll have it for your whole life and it will pay you back over and over again throughout your life. If whole life is out of your grasp, then buy term, as much as you can. The simple truth is that we never know what will happen, whether it's enjoying a family Sunday dinner one day joking about where the goofy parts in your kids come from, and having to buy a burial plot the next; or whether it's planning the family summer vacation, then finding a lump and suddenly planning treatments throughout the summer to coincide with work schedules.

"As with any insurance, life insurance is something that a person buys hoping to never use, but if the day comes that it's needed and a person doesn't have it; that's honestly a feeling I would never wish on anyone."

There really are only a couple questions I need to ask in order to make the point.

One, could needs-analysis have predicted this client's situation with both his first wife that passed away at age 31, or his current wife who suddenly got an aggressive form of breast cancer at the age of 33?

Second, which situation would the client prefer to be in? With maximum life insurance on the non-income earning spouse or something less (maybe even none)?

Insurance is not about needs that cannot be accurately predicted. It is about wants. What situation would your client want to be in? What level of protection would your client want to have if the event they are protecting against actually happens? Maximum.

Chapter 11: Principle #3 – Full Replacement of Assets Upon Death

Here is a principle that is really against the grain when it comes to traditional planning. This principle has to do with life insurance, which really should have been named "asset insurance." It should have been named asset insurance because that is what it does.

Life insurance really does not insure the value of a person's life. What is the value of a person's life? In my opinion, infinite. There is no price tag for a human life. A father, a mother, a brother or sister, a son or daughter, a grandfather or a grandmother. All human beings are priceless and of infinite worth.

When a person applies for life insurance, what do the underwriters want to know about the person, other than health? They want to know how old they are and how much money they make, or their net worth. Why? Because that is the real asset that life insurance insures. That is what is replaced when an insured dies. The purpose is to replace income or assets. I believe people would make better choices as it relates to their life insurance if they understood what it was really meant for. When talking with your clients about life insurance, I would encourage you to first teach them the purpose of it. Not the type. Not the cool strategy you have in mind. Simply teach them the purpose first.

What about insuring a non-income earning spouse or a child? Most of my clients are married couples. In those cases where one spouse does not earn an income, the question is, should that person have insurance?

Here are a few questions that might help answer the question. Usually the person that isn't working, isn't working for a reason. What is that reason? Generally, it is because they feel it's a priority to have one stay home to raise the kids. I'm not making any judgment, good or bad, right or wrong. This is a choice that the couple has made together and is something they obviously value.

Here's my question, "If Jane (the stay-at-home mom in this case) dies, who do you want to raise the kids?" Usually the answer is something like, "John. I'd want John to raise the kids." Ok, so if John, who is the income-earning spouse in this situation, is going to want to stay home and raise the kids, what's going to happen to his income? They are going to want to have it replaced. Wouldn't it be preferable in this situation to have the choice, instead of being forced to go back to work?

Here's another thing that most people don't think about. If a person loses a spouse, their best friend, their life partner, how motivated are they to go back to work next week? In the United States, it seems, we don't give people much time to mourn the loss of a loved one. The reality is, in some cases, it can take a long time. The process of mourning is healthy and important. Do we want to force people to go back to work after a loved one passes simply because they didn't have very much or any insurance on that family member?

Lastly, how is the person going to die? Again, I don't have a crystal ball that works, so, I don't know how the person is going to die. I don't know what kind of medical bills will be left behind for the surviving spouse to pay. It could be very little. It could also be millions of dollars in bills. It all depends on what led up to the death of the individual. None of which can be predicted.

Interestingly, my very first client to pass away was a 32-year-old mom. She had little kids and was married. She died in her sleep. An autopsy didn't find anything that caused the death. Prior to meeting with me, the couple didn't have any insurance on her life. Luckily, they followed my counsel and purchased life insurance on her life. Afterward, the surviving husband expressed his immense gratitude for the blessing of having the life insurance on his wife who had passed. Now he could focus on caring for and loving his children who no longer had their mom. Money didn't have to be the focus during this period of time. The kids were.

Each life insurance company has limitations on how much life insurance a non-income earning spouse can qualify for, as well as how much life insurance a person can get on their children. My recommendation is to find out what those limits are, and encourage your clients to get them, especially on the non-income earning spouse. Again, don't choose for your clients. Teach them the purpose and give them their options, and then let them choose for themselves.

We have already discussed some of the problems related to self-insuring, which is the popular approach to insuring in retirement. To reiterate the idea of self-insuring, it means that a person cancels their life insurance and then insures using their cash and investment assets instead. The opposite of that would be to own permanent life insurance that is sufficient to replace any assets that might be used/spent while both spouses are living. This is what I call Full Replacement of Assets Upon Death.

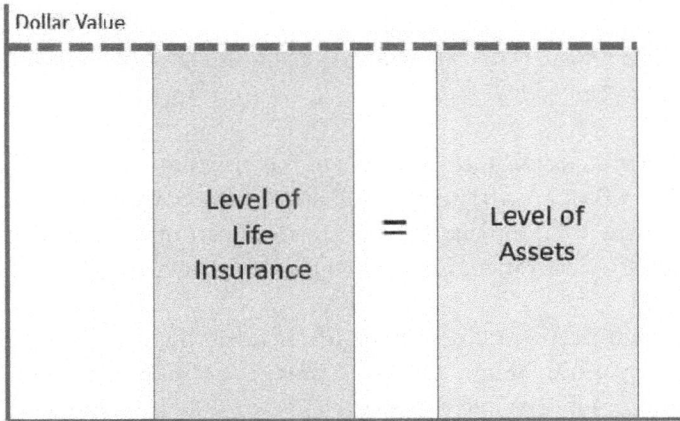

Dollar Value

Level of Life Insurance = Level of Assets

What affect would the guaranteed ability to replace any and all investment/retirement assets have on a couple in retirement? Would owning sufficient life insurance to replace any and all of a couple's assets decrease or increase their ability to utilize their assets for their intended purpose, which is retirement income?

Let's look at an example. Imagine we have two people, that we will call Jack and Larry, that are basically in the same financial position. They are both married, and they each have $1,000,000 in a 401(k).

Jack owned term life insurance prior to retirement, and then self-insured in retirement.

Larry purchased permanent life insurance, sufficient to replace all of the investment assets he owns.

Jack needs to use his assets to 1) produce income to live on, and 2) to make sure his surviving spouse also has sufficient assets to live on for the remainder of her life, if she outlives him. There are only two possible ways to guarantee that they don't run out of money before they both die.

One way is to put the money into an annuity and elect a joint lifetime income benefit from a guaranteed lifetime income rider or by annuitizing an annuity. The other way is to live on the interest only from the assets. Let's say Jack can get 4% interest per year on the money. That means the income that could be produced would be $40,000 per year.

How is Larry's situation different? He has the ability to spend down the $1,000,000 in his 401(k) over his lifetime, knowing that the day he dies, all of it will be replaced to his surviving spouse through his permanent life insurance. How does that change things?

Let's say each person retires at age 67. If Larry lived 25 more years, that would put him at age 92. Now, there is no guarantee that he will live that long. He may have a shorter lifespan, or he may, with medical advances, live even longer.

How much income could Larry take per year for 25 years? $64,012 per year.

That is 60% more income than Jack.

Why 3,000 in the years? It's just a way to show an interest-only payment
from the assets on a Payment calculator. 4% of $1,000,000 is $40,000 per year

How many retirees would like a 60% increase in income, using the same amount of assets that they currently have? It's a huge difference! The reason for the difference? One is self-insuring and the other is insuring with life insurance.

Someone who opposes this idea may say, "How in the world would the person with permanent life insurance possibly have as much in investments and retirement assets as the person who bought term life insurance and self-insures in retirement?"

First of all, what this question is assuming is that the money that Larry uses to purchase permanent life insurance is not accessible and can't be used for any additional purpose.

This is a fundamentally flawed assumption because the cash value of whole life insurance can be used at any time for any reason, including investing. This will be covered in more detail in Chapter 15.

Let's say that the money paid for permanent life insurance was simply money gone and they had no access to cash value. Let's say Larry paid $200,000 for premiums, and therefore only built $800,000 in his 401(k).

Larry now has $800,000 that can be used to produce income in retirement and spent down freely because his spouse will receive $1,000,000 from life insurance at his death. The income $800,000 could produce over a 25-year span is $51,210 per year. This is still $11,000 more (27% more income) than the self-insure strategy.

How much more money would have to be "spent" on permanent life insurance to make the incomes equal? The answer is $375,000!

Even if owning permanent life insurance did cause a $375,000 decrease in total investment assets, which person would you rather be? Would you rather be Jack, who had $1,000,000 and no life insurance, or Larry, who has $625,000 in assets and $1,000,000 in permanent life insurance?

5 Payment Calculator	— ☐ ✕

		Payment Time
Annual Payment	$40,007.48	○ Beginning-of-Year
Present Value	$625,000.00	◉ End-of-Year
Annual Interest Rate	4.00%	Known Value
Years	25.00	◉ Present Value
		○ Future Value

Here is an additional aspect to consider. How is Jack going to pay for his eventual long-term care needs? How is the person with the $1,000,000 and no life insurance going to pay for costs that currently average more than $6,000 per month nationally, when their income is only $3,333 per month?

If someone says that Jack could have bought Long-Term Care Insurance, then with the same logic, Jack must also have less money in their 401(k), and therefore less money to produce income. Also, which one has more income to buy Long-Term Care Insurance, Jack or Larry? Larry clearly has more income and has a greater ability to buy Long-Term Care Insurance.

Most likely both Jack and Larry are going to be forced to spend down their investment and retirement assets. This means that Jack's insuring strategy, the strategy he was employing to make sure their surviving spouse has sufficient funds, has a real chance of failure. In other words, Jack has a greater chance to run out of money before they run out of life.

What about the Larry? Life insurance companies have added some amazing accelerated benefit riders to permanent life insurance policies, benefits that are triggered by the inability to perform two or more of the activities of daily living (ADL's), which are dressing, toileting, continence, bathing, feeding, and transferring. The inability to perform these activities is precisely why people go into long-term care, need home health care, or go into assisted living. They do not have to use their investment and retirement assets. They can use their life insurance death benefit, or they can spend down their assets quicker.

Any way you slice it, the person with the permanent life insurance has more options, more protection, and more money. This is why the use of permanent life insurance for Full Replacement of Assets Upon Death is a fundamental principle for personal finance.

Chapter 12: Principle #4 – Six Months to One Year of Income Storage

Liquidity is a critical factor in the process of wealth creation and preservation. We've all heard the phrase "cash is king." In many ways this is true. Those that have sufficient cash at their disposal have opportunities that others do not. Those that have sufficient cash are able to avoid paying interest on unnecessary consumer debt.

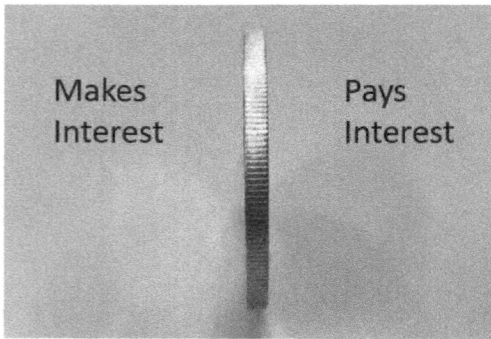

There are only two sides to the interest-rate coin. The side of paying interest, and the side of making interest. People that don't have savings are going to be on the side of paying interest throughout their lifetimes. Those that have savings are not only going to avoid wealth transfer to lenders, but they are going to be in a position to take advantage of the best investment opportunities that exist.

Consumer debt in America is an epidemic. There is a fantastic book called *Borrow: The American Way of Debt* by Louis Hyman, which I highly recommend clients and advisors read. In this book the author explains how we got to this place we find ourselves in today regarding personal consumer debt.

We live in the "now generation," where there is no deferred gratification. What we want, we want now, and we don't want to wait.

Unfortunately, lenders and easy credit have made it so that people don't really have to wait. I remember as a kid going to the store with my parents and putting things on layaway. Layaway? Most people younger than thirty right now probably have no idea what that is. It was a great concept, and a way for department stores to sell things to people who didn't quite have enough money to pay for it now. A person would select what they wanted to buy, pay whatever they could up front for it, then make payments to the store until the item was paid off.

The item was not released to the purchaser until the item was completely paid off. I don't believe layaway is even offered anymore. Why? Because credit is easy to obtain and easy to spend.

What's the cost of easy credit? As I stated earlier, consumer debt is an epidemic. American households are carrying an average credit card debt of $5,700 (based on 2019 findings by the US Census Bureau and the Federal Reserve).

Credit card interest rates, even in this very low interest-rate environment, are as high as 29%. What's interesting about this is that the same people who are carrying this credit card debt are often the people who are trying to "save" money through their retirement plans at work, mainly because of the supposed "free money" they receive in an employer match. This is the essence of the term "running in sand" from a financial perspective.

Additionally, student loan debt has gone through the roof in the United States. It is also at epidemic levels. Students are graduating from college (or not graduating in many instances) and are carrying student loan debt that is nearly impossible for them to repay. Student loan interest rates are significantly higher than they were twenty years ago, although general interest rates are at near all-time lows.

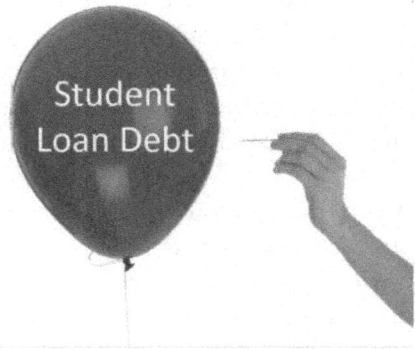

More retirees than ever are heading into retirement carrying mortgage notes on their homes. In fact, according to an article from AARP (March 26, 2018), 44% of Americans between age 60 and 70 still have a mortgage on their home when they retire.

The average savings per household in the United States is currently $8,863. That is slightly misleading, however, because only 44% of American households could pay an unexpected expense of $1,000 (CNBC article Jan 23, 2019). It is scary to see how dependent Americans are on debt to survive financially day-to-day.

It is scary to see how dependent Americans are on the low-interest rate environment, knowing that interest rates can and will raise over time going forward. It's clear that not only are most Americans not able to take advantage of the best investment opportunities that exist, but they are currently lining the pockets of financial institutions and the government at levels that have never been seen before, and they are ill-prepared for unexpected life events.

Let's shift gears to talking about "the best investment opportunities," and why high levels of liquidity are required in order to take advantage of such opportunities. A bank's primary objective is to lend money. That's where they make their money.

What factors determine when a bank chooses to lend money or refuses to lend money? Risk. The risk of the inability to repay the money, to be precise.

Another major factor is collateral. Collateral is what secures the loan. If the borrower cannot repay the loan, the bank can take possession of the collateral. In effect, collateral lowers risk. This is why collateralized loans are generally more favorable (lower interest) than uncollateralized loans. Collateral is "insurance" on the investment. Robert Kiyosaki in his book, *Who Took My Money*, said, "Most people think investing is risky. It's not investing that is risky. Investing without insurance is risky." Banks understand the importance of insuring their investments, which is why they want collateral AND insurance.

If the bank feels like the borrower has (or will have) the ability to repay the loan, and if they feel the collateral is sufficient to cover their loan, then they usually decide to lend the money to the borrower.

These same measures can help an investor identify, "the best investments." First, that the investment either has or will have the ability to repay, at a minimum, the investment basis back to the investor, and second, if things don't go as well as planned, the investor has a way out without destroying their financial future.

The worst investments are the ones that do not require collateral, that do not have anything in place to protect the investor in the event things do not go as well as hoped.

The worst investments are easy and convenient. They are pre-packaged and heavily marketed to the masses. The threshold of money required to participate is very low for the worst investments. The threshold of required knowledge and effort is also very low. The worst investments require no additional knowledge, no additional due diligence, no additional work in order to participate. The worst investments are, simply put, a gamble. As such, banks will not lend people money to invest in the worst investments. These are the reasons banks will not lend you or me money to invest in mutual funds, stocks, and other Wall Street products.

What investments will banks lend us money for? Real estate, businesses, and intellectual property.

As such, that's where the majority of millionaires have created their wealth. It's not Wall Street. In fact, according to research done by Thomas Stanley, PhD, and stated in his book, *The Millionaire Mind*, only 12% of millionaires stated that they credit "investing in the equities of public companies" as the reason for their success (p71).

This means that 88% of millionaires created their wealth in other ways, including investing in their professions (their education), their own businesses, and their own property.

All of those investments require liquidity in order to participate. All of those investments require knowledge in order to participate. All of those investments require collateral if loans are sought.

The Worst Investments	The Best Investments
Little or No Knowledge	High Level of Knowledge
Little or No Effort	A Lot of Effort (initially)
Little or No Time	A Lot of Time (initially)
Easy & Convenient	Inconvenient
Low Cash Requirement	High Cash Requirement

Why don't most financial planners talk about the best investments? The answer is money. It is important to note that advisors who are licensed to sell securities cannot get paid for selling clients their own business (or businesses), cannot get paid when their clients invest in real estate (outside of investments into REITs), and cannot get paid when clients invest in themselves, their own businesses, or their own ideas. All of this points to the blinders that securities reps have had placed on their eyes by Wall Street, which makes Wall Street products the only option for investing for their clients, which, in my view, qualify as "the worst investments."

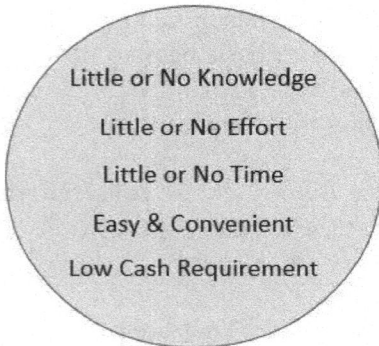

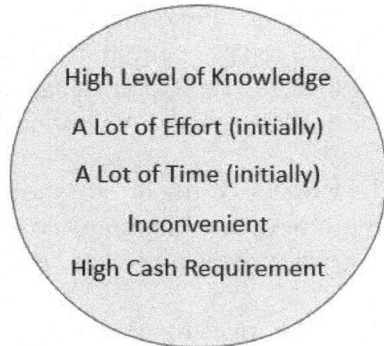

Ironically, the securities industry constantly touts themselves as being "unbiased and comprehensive." How could they be unbiased and comprehensive when they don't talk about the areas of investing that have created the most wealth for investors throughout the history of the United States and the world?

I love the fact that I have no vested interest in where my clients invest. I don't sell any investments. I teach my clients how to become real investors by encouraging them to invest in themselves and teaching them time-tested principles.

I don't have a vested interest in whether or not my clients use their money. I don't get paid more if they don't, or less if they do. Unfortunately, the securities industry can't honestly say the same. They do care where their clients invest and they do get paid less if their clients withdraw their money to live on, enjoy, or give it away to charity. The securities industry's conflict of interest is blaringly real, and they are incredibly silent about it.

Building real wealth starts with building high levels of cash. That brings us to the next question: If clients are supposed to build liquidity, where should they build it, and how much should they strive to maintain? There are not endless possibilities as to where the money can be built and maintained.

There are three qualifiers for where the money should be held. The first qualifier is that the money should be liquid. In other words, it should be in cash form. It can't be in an investment, gold, silver, stocks, horses, chickens, or mutual funds. None of those are liquid; they are investments that can and do fluctuate in value every day.

The second qualifier is that the account should be guaranteed, if possible, not only by the issuing institution but also by a government institution (i.e. FDIC, NCUA, or state life and health insurance guaranty associations). This is not the stage of wealth building where a person should take risks. The client wants to take a risk where they invest the money, not in the liquidity stage of the process.

Lastly, the money should be accessible. What good is liquidity if you cannot get to it when it is needed or wanted? With that being said, there are many different levels of accessibility. Some accounts provide immediate access, such as checking accounts. You have a debit card, you have checks, and you can even electronically transfer money directly from your checking to another person or entity by clicking a button. This is immediate and ultimate accessibility. It is also the reason checking accounts pay little or no interest and provide almost no other benefits or protections. In general, the lower the accessibility, the higher the interest will be and/or the more benefits will be attached to the account.

What are the options?
- Cash at home
- Checking
- Online checking
- Savings
- Money market accounts
- CD's
- Life insurance cash value

When we look at this list we can see that the further we move up in the list, the lower the interest and benefits, but the greater the convenience of access. The opposite is also true. As we move down the list, interest rates increase as well as benefits, but convenience of access decreases. I believe it's a valuable exercise to help clients know what all of their options are for building and maintaining cash that is guaranteed, liquid, and accessible. One isn't "better" than the other. They each serve a different purpose. Checking accounts can do things that life insurance cash value cannot, and vice versa.

Should a person have all of their liquidity in the most efficient long-term account? Of course not. People should have some of their money in the most convenient places, but if we are talking about six months of income storage, I would definitely not recommend that the majority of that is in cash in a person's house, or in a checking account at the bank. When your clients understand time value of money, they won't want that either.

Let's consider the cost of holding all of the six months of income storage in an interest-free checking account. Let's assume the client earns $100,000 per year. Six months of income storage would be $50,000. Over a 20-year period, that $50,000 is going to lose value due to inflation. At a 3% inflation rate, the $50,000 loses close to $23,000 in purchasing power.

By contrast, $50,000 in an account that earns 4% per year would be worth slightly more than $109,000. That is a pretty big difference, just based on where the money is stored.

What is the difference between the two accounts? Convenient access. One requires no time to access and use. The other might require 5-7 business days to access and use. Is the additional $59,000 in growth on the second option worth waiting a few more days to access and use? In most cases, yes. With that said, I am not promoting that all of the six months of income storage is in the most efficient long-term account. I believe people should maintain some cash at home, a certain level of funds in a checking account (probably at least one month of expenses). From there, some of the six months of income storage should probably be held in an online checking or savings account.

Right now, due to extremely low interest rates, I don't believe putting money in a money market account has any advantages over putting the money in an online savings account. Likewise, I don't believe putting money in CD's is worthwhile at this time. Those things can and will change, as interest rates do, but for now, I would not recommend those.

Last, and probably least known and understood, is the option of storing funds in the cash value of life insurance. To be clear, the account must be guaranteed, liquid, and accessible. If the life insurance policy does not have all three of those characteristics, then I would not recommend it for the purpose of liquidity.

Specifically, whole life insurance is a great long-term option for liquid income storage. The guaranteed interest on most cash value whole life insurance policies ranges from 2.5% to slightly more than 4% per year. Interest on cash value is not taxable (unless the policy is a Modified Endowment Contract). Whole life cash value is liquid, accessible, and guaranteed.

Why six months of income storage? I want to be clear that I believe that clients should have *at least* six months of income storage, and more is better. Some clients will ask, "Why not six months of expenses?" My response is, "Which one would you want if you needed the money? Six months of income, or six months of expenses?"

Most disability insurance policies, including the one that all working Americans have, Social Security Disability, have an elimination period (EP). The EP is the time between when a disability begins, and when the benefits from the disability policy begin to be paid. For Social Security disability benefits, the EP is six months. Social Security is infamous for delaying benefits, often denying benefits the first time they are applied for. The real amount of time a person may end up waiting for Social Security disability benefits could be much longer than six months.

For those few individuals who do have individual disability policies, most have either a 90-day EP or a 180-day EP (six months). The longer the EP, the lower the premium on the policy.

It's vital to be able to survive on your savings until you can start receiving benefits from disability insurance. What are other possible reasons you might need or want at least six months of income storage? Job loss, short-term income reductions, sudden large expenses, medical costs, and many other reasons. I like to ask my clients how they would feel if they had six months of their income in a guaranteed, accessible, liquid place. They always talk about how much less stress they would have, and how they feel like they would be much more prepared for the unexpected. Don't discount the importance of lowering financial stress in a person's life. Financial stress is often listed as one of the top reasons people get divorced.

In summary, clients should be encouraged to build and maintain at least six months of income storage in liquid, guaranteed, accessible places. The purpose of this is to 1) avoid unnecessary debt, 2) be prepared for the unexpected, and 3) be prepared for the best investment opportunities that exist.

If someone is going to invest, they should strive to maintain six months of income storage even after investing. In other words, if participating in an investment means that the client is going to deplete their income storage such that they are not prepared for a disability or unexpected large expense, then they should not do it.

Investing is not the priority over safety and protection. Unfortunately, there are a few clients that you will run into that absolutely can't stand having money sitting in cash anywhere, because they believe themselves to be such "amazing investors." They are overconfident, and really do not believe that anything can or will go wrong. Typically, these clients also love leveraging as much as possible, which is also something that looks great on paper, but can lead to a disastrous situation.

Have you ever heard the phrase "divide and conquer?" In finances, if you divide too much, you will be conquered. Being spread too thin, or not maintaining a high level of liquidity is a recipe for eventual failure. Liquidity is vital to building and maintaining a solid financial plan, and where it is held is secondary (but, not unimportant) to where it is held. If we are looking at long-term efficiency, which we should, then where it is held can make a big difference.

Chapter 13: Principle #5 – Velocity of Money

This is where we bring it all together.

I want to reiterate a few things that we have already discussed:

1) Financial institutions teach and promote one thing while practicing the opposite. Namely, they promote the idea that accumulation of assets leads to a person's ability to retire, while at the same time they themselves are focused on creating bigger and additional streams of revenue (cash flow).

Financial institutions promote the idea of diversification, but they themselves focus on specialization. Financial institutions promote the idea of investing in things where their customers give up knowledge and control, where they themselves would only invest in things where they are experts and where they maintain as much control as possible.

2) Wall Street has convinced people that saving and investing are the same thing, when in fact, they are different. Saving is something that should be done systematically and automatically, whereas investing should be done based on opportunity, individual situation, liquidity before and after investing, supply and demand, and many other factors.

3) Needs-based planning, or trying to predict the future needs of a client for protection and retirement, is a very weak approach to planning. Needs-based planning actually minimizes protection and does not give the client the opportunity to choose their maximum. Clients should have the right to choose their maximum, and advisors have an obligation to let them know what that is.

Predicting the amount of money a person needs in retirement, or the total value of the assets they will need in the future, is ineffective. The real purpose for the needs-based planning approach is to help financial institutions fill their coffers with people's money. Their goal is to hold on to it as long as possible and give back as little as possible. The entire "buy and hold" strategy is completely in the best interest of financial institutions and is not something they themselves utilize to create wealth.

4) A solid financial plan encourages saving as a principle, not based on circumstances. Saving is something people should do before and after retiring or reaching financial freedom. People are living longer and longer, costs for medical care are increasing, and the cost for goods and services continue to rise. All of the reasons a person should save continue throughout a person's lifetime.

A solid financial plan has the type of protection a person would want if the event they are protecting against actually happens. It has nothing to do with needs, and everything to do with what they want to have happen. Again, needs are unpredictable, and planning based on needs leads to minimization of protection in a person's plan. Needs never leads to maximum.

A solid financial plan is one that gives clients more freedom to utilize or spend their assets in retirement by having something in place that will replace whatever assets they might use, based on a guarantee and not possible, potential, hopeful rates of return. In other words, clients should have sufficient life insurance in place to replace any and all of the assets they might use in their lifetime, guaranteed.

A solid financial plan is one that has liquidity, sufficient for both emergency and opportunity. Ideally, this liquidity works as efficiently and effectively as possible throughout a client's lifetime. If we can get extra benefits, such as protection and tax-free growth and use, that is what we would want.

Finally, because clients don't have unlimited resources, it is best that their money does more than one thing for them.

Financial institutions promote one-use (or one-purpose) financial vehicles. One-use vehicles work to restrict the client's access and use of their money (i.e. penalties and fees if the funds are used for a different purpose), giving the financial institution more time to use the money for their purposes. The more uses a client can get from their money the better for them, the more benefits they can receive, the more protection they can acquire, and ultimately the more money they will have. Velocity of money is a measure of the number of uses a client gets on their money throughout their lifetime.

Let's look at velocity of money from a practical standpoint. Most people do not inherit their wealth. For most people creating wealth starts with earning money from a job. The first step to creating wealth then is to save some of what we earn.

Work and Earn

Save 15% or More

BANK

Generally, people save money in a bank product such as a checking or savings account. People should strive to have their money do all it can do, even in this stage. Thus, cash value life insurance should be considered and used in most cases if a person wants maximum efficiency over time. The purpose of this step is to build and maintain liquidity, which will position them to take advantage of opportunities as they come.

The next step is to use that money to invest in something that produces cash flow. Remember Robert Kiyosaki's definition of what an asset is, "it's something that puts money in my pocket." That is where we want to invest the money.

I'll introduce three Rules for Investing a little later, which answers the question almost everyone asks, which is "where should I invest my money?" For now, we just need to know that what we should be investing in are things that produce cash flow back to us. That could be real estate (which is a huge arena with numerous types and differences), businesses (i.e. ones that you buy, like a franchise, or ones that you start from scratch), or intellectual property (your own ideas turned into reality).

As cash flow comes back to you, your risk of loss of principal decreases, and you have additional funds that can be added to the income you are earning and saving. Then you repeat the process of having the money go into a liquid account (or liquid accounts), find/create other opportunities for investment, receive more cash flow, and repeat again. Over time, it is possible that the amount of money you are saving will actually be higher than your entire income from your job or profession. In fact, that is the eventual goal, and would be the point of financial freedom.

This is the process by which most millionaires and billionaires are created. It is not by "saving" money into retirement plans and hoping the balance grows ("compounds") over time.

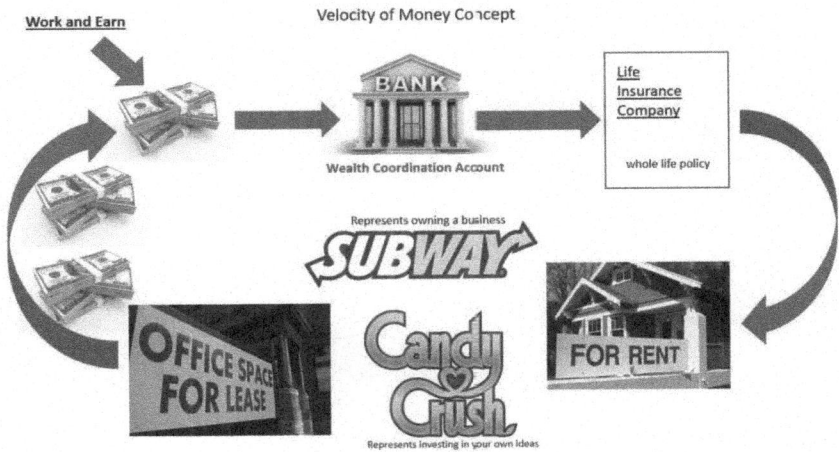

Part IV: Financial Products

Chapter 14: Financial Products

Even though we understand that financial institutions are in it for their own best interests and that they create products and promote strategies that are designed for their gain and not ours so much, we still need and want them.

Financial institutions can do things that we, as individuals, cannot do on our own. Financial institutions deal with hundreds of thousands to millions of people. Volume matters. Certain things that financial institutions can do to create wealth and benefits are not in the realm of possibility for most individuals (outside of the wealthiest few in the world).

Financial institutions use an economic principle called The Law of Large Numbers. The Law of Large Numbers states that the greater the population in the sample, the more predictable certain outcomes are. For example, if an insurance company only insured ten people, there is a greater possibility that they will not be able to predict how many in that group are going to die early, acquire certain illnesses, etc. However, the insurance company's ability to predict such things increases as the number of people they insure increases.

The Law of Large Numbers allows insurance companies to invest huge blocks of money and maintain a certain level of liquidity with more certainty, because they can predict how many people are going to die, become sick, etc.

Banks use the Law of Large numbers as well, but for a different purpose. Everyone knows that if all depositors of a bank went to the bank today to withdraw their funds that the bank would not have nearly enough money on hand to pay everyone the amounts they have on deposit.

Banks are required (and want) to maintain a certain level of liquidity, which is more than enough to cover any of the bank's usual transactions for a day (withdrawals, etc.). This level of liquidity is called a "reserve." The more people they have banking at the financial institution, the more accurate they will be in determining how much money people will use each day. The rest is invested through lending or other ventures. Banks can only exist because of the Law of Large numbers. If they had to keep all of the money deposited in their accounts liquid, they could not make enough money to survive.

Because financial institutions have the capability of doing things that we cannot do as individuals, we can benefit from them and the products that they create for our use. Are those products designed to be profitable to the financial institutions? Absolutely! Is that a bad thing? Of course not! Making a profit on something is not evil, unless it is done deceptively or injuriously.

If a business produces a product or service that I value more than the dollars in my wallet, and I trade my dollars for their product or service, I want them to make a profit. Why? Because I want them to continue to be in business. I want them to continue to be in business because I value the product or service they provide. If I do not want them to make money, then I am expecting people to work and take risks simply out of goodness in their hearts, which unfortunately does not put food on the table for them.

I get asked all of the time what my preferred client looks like. One of the defining characteristics of my preferred client is one that wants me to make money. If a client does not want me to make money I don't want him/her as a client. In that same vein, we want financial institutions that make products and services that we value to stay in business and not only survive but profit.

Financial products are simply tools that are designed for different purposes, just like tools on a toolbelt. It's good to have different tools. A hammer does a certain job. A Phillips screwdriver does a certain job. A paint brush does another job, and so on.

I find it comical when I hear the "financial gurus" say things like "whole life is a terrible product" or "annuities are garbage." That is like saying a flathead screwdriver is a piece of junk and has no value, or that table saw is worthless. Every financial product is designed for a purpose. If a person does not understand or value the purpose of the financial tool, that's for them to decide, but to make blanket statements that a certain tool is simply garbage is foolish.

In the next three chapters, I will expound on three of the controversial financial products: mutual funds, annuities, and life insurance.

Chapter 15: Mutual Funds

What is a mutual fund? Is it an investment? Sort of. A mutual fund is a bunch of investors who pool their money together to be invested by a fund manager. The largest funds have millions of individual and institutional investors and manage hundreds of billions in assets.

A mutual fund is not actually the investment. It is the way through which people invest, but in a strange way, it is also an investment because it has share values that are based on the combined values of the underlying investments (usually stocks and/or bonds) that the mutual fund owns.

Mutual funds are super convenient for people because they don't require a large initial investment to participate and are usually available through an employer-sponsored retirement plan. For most funds, you can invest as little as $50 or $100 to start. You don't even have to buy full shares; you can buy portions of shares.

A mutual fund is the sole ready-buyer and seller of their own shares. In other words, if you owned a piece of land and you wanted to sell it, you would have to find a buyer before you could sell it. That could take a lot of time and effort. With mutual funds, you can buy or sell any time, and the fund itself will buy back the fund share. Because the seller is selling the mutual fund shares, the mutual fund itself isn't necessarily selling the underlying stock or bond investments. So, although the underlying investments (the underlying stocks and bonds) the mutual fund owns and the fund shares are tied on a string, there is leeway for the fund to cash out investors and not necessarily sell an equivalent amount of underlying investments.

Mutual funds are THE WAY most of America is investing in the stock market. Most Americans invest via their employer sponsored retirement plan (usually a 401(k)). Most Americans invest automatically through payroll deductions into their retirement plans. Mutual funds and Wall Street in general have successfully lobbied to make it ultra-convenient for Americans to invest in the stock market through employer-sponsored retirement plans and convenient payroll deductions.

More recently, the Wall Street lobby has been successful at passing regulations and laws allowing for automatic enrollment for qualifying full-time employees. In other words, you don't even have to choose to participate, the choice is made for you. Thankfully, however, the law still gives employees the option to opt out of contributing. My guess is that that will change over time. We already have precedent for forced contributions in many government-run employee retirement plans. If Wall Street gets their way, all full-time employees will be forced to contribute, without the ability to opt out, sort of like Social Security Retirement.

There has been a lot of talk over the past few decades about privatizing Social Security Retirement. What does that mean? It means that instead of running Social Security like a Defined Benefit Pension (which is what it is like currently), it would look more like 401(k)'s do, where people have a choice (the selling point) in how their money is invested, but all of the guarantees would come off. No guaranteed income amount, no guarantee that you could not outlive the income, and so on. No guarantees.

Unfortunately, there are many Americans who think they can grow their Social Security better without the guarantees in the market. These are the same types of people who thought it would be better for their employers to offer 401(k)'s where the employees could "manage" their own money and choose how it's invested, versus relying on guaranteed defined benefit pension plans. How has that worked out? Not well at all.

However, it was a big win for employers and Wall Street. Likewise, privatizing Social Security would be a big win for the Federal Government (relieving them of their obligations – guarantees of income payments) and Wall Street. The big loser in both cases would be the investor.

Imagine from Wall Street's point of view how valuable it would be to have all of the dollars that are currently going into Social Security Retirement instead go into their funds? Of course they want that to happen! The question is, is this the best option for individual

Americans? Take away all of the guarantees and give the responsibility to invest to people who admit themselves that they don't know what they're doing and have no control?

What is the purpose of mutual funds? It is to make investing easy and convenient. The purpose is to have someone else manage a person's investment decisions instead of doing it themselves.

Who do mutual funds appeal to? People that do not want to do the investment research and work themselves. In other words, it appeals to the laziness in people. "I don't want to come home from work and then do more work. I want to pay an expert to manage my money for me." It's the idea that a person can go to work, 9 to 5, come home, do yard work and watch a game, and then repeat this process, and somehow retire financially-free at the magic age of 65 or 67.

How popular is mutual fund investing? In 1929 mutual funds didn't really exist. Investing in the stock market was done almost exclusively by the extremely wealthy. Only about 10% of Americans had investments in the stock market in 1929. Today, according to a recent Gallup poll, about 55% of Americans have money invested in the stock market. The reason? The ease, convenience, and extreme marketing of mutual funds.

So, what's so bad about mutual funds? Let's go back to the rules of financial institutions.

They want our money (check).

They want it on a regular and ongoing basis (check).

They want to hold our money as long as possible (check).

They want to give back as little as possible (check).

Do mutual funds, and how they are marketed, achieve these objectives for the financial institutions selling them. Absolutely. Mutual funds are sold to the masses. They promote the idea that through convenience and ignorance you can invest and retire financially free one day.

They promote the idea that through diversification and asset allocation you can mitigate whatever risks the stock market poses over time. They promote the idea that the stock market always goes up, conveniently ignoring the fact that sometimes it goes down over significant periods of time (periods of 10 plus years). They conveniently side-step the fact that the market isn't always up when people need it, and that most have lost huge portions of their investment accounts when the market "corrects" (which is a nice way of saying it dropped significantly).

They promote the idea that it's always the right time to buy, through a fancy term they call "dollar-cost averaging." They promote the idea that it is never the right time to sell, even at this time when the market is at its all-time high. Just throw the buy-low sell-high idea in the trash. Somehow that doesn't apply to the stock market, and certainly doesn't apply to mutual funds, because they are expertly managing your money. They know when to buy and sell, and you don't. So, trust them. They promote the buy-at-all-prices and hold forever strategy. I cannot think of anything they could possibly come up with that would be better for their bottom lines than to convince the American people that somehow this is true.

If you want to know how bad it is, I recommend watching two very good documentaries on the subject: *The Retirement Gamble* (PBS Frontline) and *The Inside Job* (by Charles Ferguson). *The Retirement Gamble* does a great job pointing out the problems associated with actively managed mutual funds (any mutual fund that is not an index fund). It talks about the extreme and complex fees that mutual funds charge.

In an article written by Kenneth Kim, a Forbes Contributor, September 24, 2016, Mr Kim lays out the average unhidden and hidden costs of mutual funds. His article reports findings from various research studies done by some well-known universities and research institutions (i.e. University of Virginia, Virginia Tech, Financial Analyst Journal Study, Morningstar, and others). Most people have no idea that mutual funds charge something different than the "expense ratio" they publish in their seldom-read prospectuses.

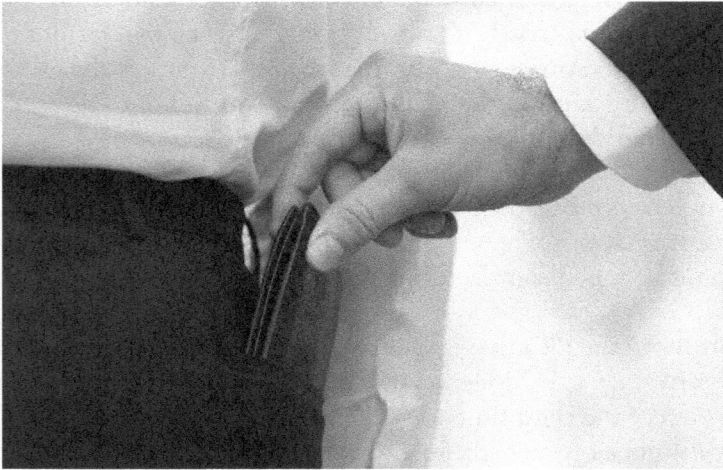

Let me correct that. Most people have no idea that they are being charged, let alone what those charges might be. Very few people ever read the prospectus, and even if they did, they likely wouldn't understand what they read. To prove my point, I'll quote a few lines from the book, *Take on the Street*. In it, Arthur Levitt, a former SEC Chairman (top regulator of the securities industry), states:

As I pored over fund prospectuses, what really got under my skin was that the documents were impossible to understand. At first I was embarrassed. Then it hit me: if someone with twenty-five years in the securities business coudn't decipher the jargon, imagine the frustration for the average investor. Mutual fund prospectuses were written in impenetrable legalese, by and for the securities lawyers. I would soon discover that this was but one of the troubling practices in the mutual fund industry.

According to the research findings Mr. Kim wrote about, the average disclosed mutual fund fees amount to 1.19% per year. The undisclosed fees add up to 5.03% per year. Note that some of those fees, for example, the "costs due to tax inefficiency" would not apply to people owning mutual funds in qualified plans or IRA's.

In a great article written by Fortune regarding a letter by Warren Buffet to Berkshire Hathaway shareholders ("Cut Your Gains", Fortune, March 20, 2006), Mr Buffet explains that even if the stock market does get "historical" rates of return, the average investor will do much worse because of the fees that Wall Street charges.

In another book, *The Smartest Investment Book You'll Ever Read*, the author, Daniel R. Solin, writes about the performance of actively managed funds versus passively managed, and subsequently significantly lower cost, funds. He quotes research done by a friend of his, Edward S. O'Neal, PhD, who was an associate dean for the Babcock Graduate School of Management at Wake Forrest University. After researching nearly 500 actively managed mutual funds, which had as their objective to beat the S&P 500, only two percent of them actually did over the timeframe, from 1998 through 2003. In other words, the odds were extremely low that someone would pick one of the ten mutual funds that were successful.

This research proves a few things. First, even the smartest, highest-paid people in the world cannot predict the right times to buy or sell in the stock market. Second, most mutual funds charge high fees and underperform their benchmark indexes.

People are investing blindly into mutual funds. Most don't know even the slightest bit of important information about the funds they are investing in. They simply look at the name of the fund (i.e. Global Emerging Markets), look at the past few years' average rates of return and make a choice.

In more than twenty years in the financial planning business I have never met a single person that knew the name of any of the fund managers where he/she had money invested. Not one. This is something that is extremely easy to find out but illustrates just how willfully ignorant so many are regarding investment into mutual funds, and how powerful the follow-the-crowd mentality is.

What people are doing is not really investing, it is gambling. They are gambling with their futures. They are gambling with hard-earned money, and for what reason? Because it's common. It's because most people are also doing it, which somehow makes it ok.

If you ask those same people if they trust Wall Street, what will they say? They do not. If you asked those same people if they would write a check for tens of thousands of dollars to someone that they do not know, who would invest the money for them, would they? They say they would not. Yet, they are.

That is what I have against mutual funds and Wall Street. It is that they are promoting laziness. They are promoting ignorance. They are lying to people about what they charge. They constantly ignore and fail to disclose their conflicts of interest. Ultimately, gambling is a loser's game, and the house always wins. The average Joe is a pawn in the Wall Street system, not the beneficiary. Time has proven this.

We have now seen more than 50 years of mutual funds being the predominant investment vehicle for most Americans. What has it produced? If saving some money is the goal, it has sort of worked (it's been offset mostly by consumer debt), but if creating financial independence (or retirement) is the goal, then it has failed miserably.

According written by Nerd Wallet contributor Arielle O'Shea, "A record number of 401(k) holders at Fidelity Investments hit millionaire status in 2018. Not one of them? You are in very good company: A seven-figure 401(k) balance is the exception, not the rule. In fact, the average 401(k) balance at Fidelity – which holds 16.2 million 401(k) accounts and is consistently ranked as the largest defined contribution record-keeper – was $103,700 as of March 2019. If that still seems high, consider that averages tend to be skewed by outliers, and in this case, that number is being propped up by those rare millionaires. The median, which represents the middle balance between highs and lows, is just $24,500."

Some might say that is a misrepresentation because it includes all ages. So, let's just look at 60-69year-olds. According to the same article, the average 401(k) balance for this group is $195,500, and the median is $62,000. We are near the end of what is the longest bull-run in the stock market's history. We're definitely not looking at a cherry-picked terrible period of time. We are looking at arguably the best period of time, and yet, the results speak for themselves. It's pitiful. It's not working. People are not better off, at least outside of Wall Street fund managers.

When I look at my own experience over twenty years, meeting with hundreds of people for financial planning, I have never once seen a situation where a person could replace their pre-retirement income with income from their mutual funds and IRA's.

Not even close.

Now, I do know of people who are retired, and the way they invested was through the stock market, mainly through mutual funds. However, when you take a deeper dive into their situation you find that they were often highly compensated executives of corporations, participated in deferred compensation plans, and more often than not, they have received Restricted Stock Units that in most cases significantly exceeds the value they have in their 401(k)'s and IRA's that they contributed to themselves.

In other words, they aren't able to retire because of their own investing prowess in the stock market, or because they had a 401(k), or because they received a match, or because they invested in stocks, bonds, or mutual funds in or outside of their IRA's. It's because they were highly compensated employees of corporations and received extra benefits that the average Joe would not receive. However, you will find that these same people are some of the biggest proponents (outside of those selling securities) of investing in the market and saving through 401(k)'s and IRA's, because "it worked for them". When you ask them how they did it, they will say that they happened to be in the right place (worked for the right company) at the right time, and just as easily could have been the opposite. They didn't have control over it (other than that they saved money). They were not experts at investing.

Bottom line, products and strategies that promote ignorance and laziness are ripe for the picking for Wall Street managers, and do not create financial independence for the average Joe. Mutual funds are designed to be part of the Accumulation Theory. The focus of a mutual fund is not to produce income, even if the mutual fund states that its purpose is to invest in Dividend and Income stocks. Dividend and Income stock just means that they invest in more "stable companies" that have been around a long time. It does not mean they are trying to create the largest cash flow to the investor.

For more valuable information about mutual funds and their tactics, I recommend reading *Take on the Street*, by Arthur Levitt.

Chapter 16: Annuities

Annuities are a unique financial tool that is often maligned by supporters of Wall Street, which isn't surprising because more money going to annuities means less money going to them. Annuities are designed to do one thing better than any other pre-packaged financial product, and that is to produce income.

They are not primarily a vehicle designed to grow a person's money, although they can and do, sometimes much more effectively than stock market products. Annuities have inherent tax benefits associated with them, namely tax-deferred growth. As we have already discussed, however, tax-deferral may not always be the best strategy (i.e. if taxes are going to increase over time).

There are three major types of annuities, fixed, fixed index, and variable. All annuities are issued and sold by insurance companies that have the financial backing to support the annuity guarantees.

Variable annuities are the least guaranteed. The money in a variable annuity is invested in mutual funds, and therefore can increase or decrease in value over time. The only advantages of a variable annuity versus simply investing in mutual funds directly is that of tax-deferral (the money that can be invested each year is not limited like IRA's) and lifetime income payments, either through annuitization or lifetime income riders. Unfortunately, the advantages of variable annuities are often offset by the myriad of charges in these types of accounts. Because of the poor performance of variable annuities, you rarely find them in the marketplace anymore.

Fixed annuities are basically glorified CD's. They offer a fixed interest rate, which is determined at the beginning of the contract. These accounts are fully guaranteed, but most of them only offer two ways to withdraw money. The first way is through partial withdrawals. The second way is through annuitization. Annuitization is basically the transfer of an asset to the insurance company in return for a guaranteed lifetime income (over single or a joint life). There is no turning back from this decision. Once annuitized, the owner cannot access any more capital from the account even if they need to. They only have access to the income that is guaranteed to be paid out, and nothing more. As people are living longer and longer, and unexpected financial issues arise because of it, annuitization is a little bit of a scary proposition for such a long period of uncertainty.

Fixed index annuities combine the certainty of protection against loss and guaranteed lifetime income, with the ability to retain access to the balance in the account if and when needed. Fixed index annuities give the owner the opportunity to earn higher rates of interest (albeit not guaranteed to do so) than bank and credit union products and fixed annuities.

They do this by offering what are called "index crediting strategies." It is important to note that the money invested in an index annuity is not invested in the stock market. Like a fixed annuity, the money is invested in the general account of the insurance company. Instead of guaranteeing an interest rate, the insurance company allows the investor to decide which crediting strategies he/she wants to follow. The choices are usually following various indexes (i.e. S&P 500, Russell 2000, etc.), and are annual point to point, bi-annual point to point, or monthly point to point.

They may also have caps (limits on how high they can go), participation rates (how much of the gain do they get as a percentage), or a margin (how much does the index have to gain before the account earns anything). The good thing with any of these strategies is that none of them exposes the owner to potential loss, regardless of how the market performs.

Personally, I believe all employer-sponsored retirement plans should offer index annuities as an option. Most people participating in retirement plans admit they have very little knowledge or control in the stock market and would prefer an option that does not expose them to loss but gives them the opportunity to earn more than a fixed rate.

When it comes time to retire and start taking income from the retirement plan, most plans do not have an option to create any sort of guaranteed income for the account owner. For this reason, they have to move the money from the plan when they retire in order to create income. Why not have it already built in the plan as an option? They do not offer it because Wall Street doesn't want them in the plans. The more money that goes into annuities, the less will go into Wall Street products.

The 2018 Retirement Confidence Survey (by EBRI) found that 4 of 5 workers are interested in an option that provides guaranteed income for life. Yet, none of them have that option in their retirement plans.

Whenever I present Index Annuities as an option to clients, they almost always say something like, "Why are so many people opposed to annuities? They sound like a good option."

Why is Ken Fisher (investment analyst and the founder and chairman of Fisher Investments) opposed to annuities? The answer is that they don't want money going anywhere but in their pockets. Wall Street has a monopoly on financial advertising and marketing, and they aren't about to let insurance companies into the game if they can help it.

I believe a major reason for the push for the DOL Rule (pass in 2016) was actually to delegitimize and malign fixed index annuities and anyone who sold them. This wasn't the marketed reason for the rule. The marketed reason was so that advisors would be required to do things in the best interest of the client, which absolutely should be the case every time. The problem is you cannot regulate people into being honest and ethical.

Advisors that are unethical are still going to find ways to be unethical no matter how many rules and regulations that are imposed on them. Can you think of any industry that is more heavily regulated than Wall Street? Yet, dishonesty, unethical conduct, and selfish ambition runs rampant.

In the documentary Inside Job (Ferguson) it shows part of a congressional hearing in which a congressman asks Lloyd Blankfein, who was and still is a top executive for Goldman Sachs, if he thought it was ok to recommend clients buy offerings that they were calling "a piece of crap" behind closed doors and then betting against the clients who buy it.

Lloyd replied that he thought it was just fine "in the context of market making." Sorry Lloyd, lying and stealing is never ok. I'm sure your mother taught you that. What is really sad about this situation is that people like Lloyd are still the ones in power. They are still the ones in charge of Wall Street, which is why I do not trust them.

After 2008, when all of their misdeeds were uncovered, and people like Michael Lewis exposed them, they were effectively given a hand slap, and went back to work. No real punishment. The SEC, which sold out to people like Lloyd Blankfein, turned their heads and took bribes, according to the documentary. Ratings agencies that are supposed to be in the business of helping protect the consumer, sold out too. None of the bad guys went to jail. Stuff like that is reserved usually for small fries that they can use as a demonstration. They certainly don't want to upset the entire applecart to make their point, which is what they would have done had they penalized the big players like they should have. Watch the documentaries.

I love when anti-annuity people say something about the "high fees" or "high commissions" associated with annuities. They always act like they are coming from a fee-free benevolent land of investing that supposedly they promote to their clients. I like recent ads from brokerages saying things like "If you don't get paid, neither do we." What a load! Total and complete false advertising. Name one stock brokerage that only makes money if their investors do. They do not exist. They all get paid whether their investors make money or not. Now, it is true, if their investors' accounts grow, so does their income. I am not disagreeing with that, but trying to convince people that they only get paid if their investors make money is a complete lie. I'm not sure how the SEC can allow that sort of advertising.

Let's talk about fees on annuities. Generally, there are only fees on a fixed index annuity if it has a rider, such as a nursing home rider, guaranteed lifetime income rider, or flexible withdrawal rider.

All annuities also have potential surrender charges (charges that only occur if the client pulls money out earlier than the account is designed to do). When an investor moves money into an index annuity, the insurance company doesn't subtract any costs from the value of the account up front, even though there are costs associated with the creation of the product, selling the product (commissions), and so on. It takes the insurance company years to recoup those costs.

If the insurance company is not going to subtract those costs from the clients' accounts, then they have to recoup the costs over time by investing the money. The potential surrender charge is there just in case the client decides to pull money out before the end of the surrender period (the time the insurance company needs to hold on to the money in order to make it profitable). If the client pulls money out early, they pay a surrender charge. Typically, those charges start out anywhere from 7-10% and then decrease over the surrender period until they are gone entirely. The fees for lifetime income riders usually are somewhere around .75 to 1.5% per year, which are significantly lower than fees associated with most actively managed mutual funds, for which mutual funds provide no guarantees or added benefits.

Let's talk about commissions. Most index annuities pay commissions from 3% to 7% one-time. Sometimes they offer a trailing commission on products, if the advisor wants to choose that instead of the one-time higher commission. These commissions, over any significant period of time, absolutely pale in comparison to the trailing commissions securities reps and brokerages receive and are subtracted from the clients' accounts. It's not even close! It's really just a marketing tactic to badmouth the insurance industry, plain and simple.

At the end of the day annuities can be a great tool in a person's plan. Like most financial tools, annuities are not for everyone or every situation, but they offer unique features and benefits that no other financial product can, and the truth is, most people want those benefits.

Chapter 17: Life Insurance

It is hard to believe that life insurance is a controversial financial tool, but it absolutely is, especially whole life insurance. There are three major types of life insurance: term, universal, and whole life.

Term life insurance is temporary life insurance. It was not designed by the insurance companies to be owned for a very long period of time, especially after age 60. Term life insurance is generally owned through work, or group term life insurance. The premiums are low, so people equate that to being cheap. If paying a relatively low amount of money into something and never getting anything back is cheap, then it's cheap.

I think it is important to define the word "cost." Is the definition for "cost" the amount of money I put into something? If so, my bank account costs me the most money, because my entire paycheck goes into my bank account, but that's not the real definition for "cost" is it? The real definition for the word "cost" is input minus output.

In other words, if I put $5 into something and I get $6 back, it really didn't cost me anything. In fact, I made money. However, if I put $5 into something and get nothing back, then it cost me $5.

I'm not saying that I don't get anything for my term life insurance premium. I certainly do. I get the peace of mind that comes from knowing that if I die, then not only does my beneficiary get all that I have paid into the policy, but many multiples more. However, if at any point I decide to cancel the policy, or I lose it because I no longer work for the employer offering the benefit, then everything I have paid into the policy is lost. I don't get any premiums back. In that case, it cost me everything I paid into it. I'm not saying it's not worth having the protection. It *absolutely* is, but is there a better way to own life insurance long-term?

Term life insurance is designed to have the lowest premium up front (the lowest of any type of life insurance) but over time increases exponentially. The increasing premium is designed to squeeze people out of the policy over time (to cancel it at some point before they die). The insurance companies are very successful at this. I have read various statistics over the years showing anywhere from 90% to 99% of term policies never result in a death claim.

Term life insurance certainly has a place in most people's financial plans, especially those that believe in the principle of maximum protection. However, the reality is that most term insurance policies are not going to be in force when a person dies. Term is temporary, and if a person only uses term life insurance, they will self-insure at some point, which is the most-costly way to insure.

Universal life insurance is designed to have a lower required premium than whole life, while still providing many of the benefits of permanent life insurance. It is important to note, however, that universal life insurance is not a fully guaranteed contract. Based on conversations I have had with actuaries who create these products, universal life insurance must be overfunded and "babysat" (words from an actuary I know well who creates this product) in order to last a person's lifetime. However, they are not sold by most life insurance agents that way.

They are generally sold with the idea that the premiums are flexible, and that the client is only required to pay a certain amount (a minimum required amount) in order to have it. They are often sold with the idea that the cash value is going to somehow outperform their more "expensive" counterpart, whole life insurance, even though the cash value of universal life has exponentially increasing costs ("costs of insurance") that are drawn out monthly or annually.

Many of the new universal life policies have added "no-lapse guarantees" to the policies, which basically state that if the cash value is insufficient to pay the monthly costs of insurance, that the policy will remain in force for a period of time. I have never seen a no-lapse guarantee longer than twenty years or past age 67. Most of the no-lapse guarantees are ten years. After the no-lapse guarantee period, universal life policies will only stay in force only if the cash value is sufficient to pay the ever-growing costs of insurance within the policy.

Universal life insurance is never actually owned (it is never paid-up). Generally, illustrations for universal life insurance can also be manipulated by the agent and are allowed to show rates of growth up to a maximum limit, which I believe is currently 7.25% per year. Agents don't have any such control over whole life illustrations. Whole life insurance illustrations are only allowed to show the Current Dividend and Interest, and the Guaranteed (worst-case scenario). Will the client get 7.25% because the agent showed them that on their illustration? No. So, why do agents show those rates? Because it makes the policy look better than whole life. It's mathematics, not real money. Again, the only thing right about projections and illustrations is that they are all wrong.

I personally believe that universal life insurance appeals to the get something for nothing crowd and are generally sold as a part of the Accumulation theory of wealth creation.

Universal Life appeals to agents who focus mainly on selling large single premiums (or large premiums for short periods of time – i.e. 5-10 years) as a part of a corporate bonus, executive bonus, key person, or captive insurance program because universal life allows much larger dump-in premiums than whole life before becoming a MEC (Modified Endowment Contract – a taxable account).

It seems the insurance agents are constantly trying to find ways to deduct the premium and retain the tax-free nature of the policy. Tax-free going in and tax-free going out. It seems like none of these strategies have really panned out well for people over time, becauseit is not the life insurance they are selling, it is the tax-deductible contribution and tax-free distribution that they are selling.

For anyone considering selling the idea of captive insurance companies, I would highly recommend the book *The Definitive Guide to Captive Insurance Companies*, by Peter Strauss, Esq. as well as obtaining advice from a qualified tax-attorney (and not one that sells the captive insurance strategy). As appealing as the idea may sound of huge sums of money going into a plan/strategy that can be deducted from taxes and eventually come back tax-free, I would emphasize the caution that Mr. Strauss expresses repeatedly in his book that the captive insurance company actually be, as its primary purpose, insurance. If the primary purpose is really tax deductions and tax-free withdrawals, the IRS will see through the scheme, and I believe your client will be sorry.

Finally, I don't think I have ever seen a universal life insurance illustration shown without the agent trying to demonstrate unending policy loans from the policy supposedly without causing the policy to cancel. However, if the net cash value is insufficient to pay the exponentially growing costs of insurance in the policy, it will lapse. If the policy lapses, and the policy owner has taken a lot of "tax-free" policy loans, those loans suddenly are forgiven, and anything received above the total after-tax premiums paid will be taxable. Imagine if a client follows this advice, takes large policy loans year after year in retirement, thinking that they are tax-free, and then the policy cancels? What will the client feel about the idea, strategy, or you at that time? All I can say is I hope you have great E&O coverage. At the end of the day, I don't believe in getting something for nothing, and I believe those trying to get something for nothing will ultimately pay the higher price. Isn't it enough that life insurance is already given the most favorable tax treatment of any financial product? I am perfectly satisfied with that reality.

The last major type of life insurance is whole life. I don't think any financial tool has been badmouthed more than this product, nor is there a financial product that has been more consistent and reliable, not just over a few decades, but more than a hundred years! Does it deserve the hate? Let's break it down and take a closer look.

Whole life insurance is a product that has been around relatively unchanged for hundreds of years. It is a fairly simple product. Although the required premium for whole life insurance starts higher than any other type, it is guaranteed to stay level for life (thus the name, "whole life").

It has a death benefit that is guaranteed as long as the premium is paid, no matter how long the person lives. It also can be changed to a Reduced Paid-Up policy, which means the death benefit can be reduced to the amount of the coverage that is paid for (owned) and no further premiums are due. It has a cash value (similar to the way equity builds in a house) that grows in the policy, generally at a rate of 3-4% guaranteed per year.

The best way to look at the cash value is that it is the amount of death benefit that is currently available for the policyowner to use. The reason I say it that way is because if a person takes a cash value loan and then dies while the cash value loan is outstanding, the loan is subtracted from the death benefit (because it has already been paid out).

The cash value of a whole life insurance policy is contractually guaranteed to exceed the premiums paid (with the exception of some policies that are started after age 70), and eventually will equal the death benefit. Because the cash value will exceed the premiums paid, and because the cash value is accessible at any time for any reason by the policyowner, the life insurance eventually has no cost to it.

I did not say "no premium," I said no cost (cost = input minus output). In addition, whole life insurance that is issued by mutual insurance companies (life insurance companies owned by the "participating" whole life policyholders) receive profit from the life insurance company in the form of dividends. The dividends paid to policyholders are not taxable if they are reinvested in the policy, as they are considered "a return of premium" by the IRS.

Dividends are the only non-guaranteed factor in a whole life policy. With that said, I do not know of any whole life insurance company that has ever *not* paid a dividend, with most of them being more than a hundred years old.

Why do certain supposed financial gurus hate it? They say things like, it is a "high commission policy" and that's the only reason agents sell it, or they say "it's a bad investment," or they say, "it's too expensive," or they say that people could "buy term and invest the difference" and do much better. All of these statements are very misleading or untrue. Let me address each one.

The commission on a whole life policy is generally 50% to 100% of the first-year premium. That does sound high without digging a little deeper into the subject and making a proper comparison. There is a big range depending on each carrier's agent contract. Typically, the insurance companies who deal with traditional "general agencies" have a base commission of 50% to the agent. The rest of the commission goes to the general agent.

Insurance companies that don't use the traditional general agency format pay somewhere from 80-100% commission on the first-year premium. By the way, the commission percentages are basically the same for term and universal life. Also, it's important to note that I am talking about the commission on the "base required premium," not any riders such as a Paid-Up Rider (PUR). Typically the commission on PUR Riders are around 3-5%.

Let's do a comparison with a mutual fund. Let's say someone starts a whole life policy with a $10,000 annual base premium. The commission would be as much as $10,000. The client, let's say a 35-year-old male, would get about $1,000,000 death benefit for that amount of premium. Subsequent commissions on subsequent premiums are generally 3-5% of the annual premium. In other words, in year two, the commission on the $10,000 base premium would be only as much as $500.

Let's say the same $10,000 could go into a mutual fund that only charges 1% per year. The first-year commission to the mutual fund salesman will only be $100. However, over a 32-year period, if the mutual fund grew at a rate of 6% per year, the commission from the mutual fund to the fund representative will exceed $107,000. In comparison the life insurance agent would have only received $25,500 in commissions over the same 32-year period.

The fund representative gets paid commission on the entire balance in the account each year. He/she gets paid commissions on amounts of money they already got paid commissions on the year before. They get paid commissions on top of commissions on top of commissions. The only thing really compounding in a mutual fund is the commission to the securities representative. By contrast, the life insurance agent only gets paid a commission on the annual premium (once on each premium paid). That's a huge difference! Who gets paid the "high commission?" If we compare the life insurance agent to the securities representative, the securities representative's commissions are significantly higher. There is really no comparison.

"Whole life insurance is a bad investment." True, but only because it is not an investment at all. It is also not a retirement account. It is a fully guaranteed insurance product. No investment is fully guaranteed. Investments have risk of loss of principal associated with them. Whole life insurance does not.

Whole life insurance is insurance with a guaranteed liquid cash account (cash value). What should whole life insurance be compared with if not investments? It should be compared with other types of life insurance and possibly other guaranteed liquid savings tools.

If we compare it to other liquid savings tools, over time whole life insurance is going to outperform the competition. Why? Two reasons; first it has a higher interest rate (as I said previously, the guaranteed interest rate is typically 3-4% per year), and second is that it grows tax-free (technically it is "tax-deferred," but it is tax-free as long as it is a non-MEC policy and the cash is only used in the form of policy loans).

For example, let's say we have a 35-year old who is saving $10,000 per year into a bank account earning 2% per year. After 32 years the account will have $442,270 in cash.

By contrast, if that same person put the $10,000 per year into a whole life policy, based on the current dividend scale of one of the existing reputable mutual life insurance companies I work with, the cash value would be $557,031. Not only would the life insurance have more cash, but it would also have a death benefit of $1,150,000 and would not have been taxable like the savings account would have been.

Additionally, if the person chose the strategy with the savings account instead of the whole life insurance, he would likely have spent money on term life insurance, which, if we are going to do a proper comparison, would have to be subtracted from the gains in the savings account. If an equivalent term life insurance policy had a premium of $400 per year and was level for 32 years (which is quite an understatement for what the real premium would be),the person would have spent more than $12,800 in term life insurance premiums over the same period. It is very clear that the person with whole life insurance would have more cash and better long-term protection, even with the supposed "high commission" considered.

What about "investing the difference?" Wouldn't it be better to buy term life insurance and invest the difference? The people promoting this idea don't really understand what a person can or can't do with whole life insurance.

First, no one ever calculates "the difference" and invests that. If a person buys term life insurance, they save what they were going to save anyway. They do not consider any sort of difference between term life insurance and whole life insurance. "Buy term and invest the difference" is a marketing phrase by people selling term and Wall Street securities.

As a reminder, whole life insurance is not an investment, and the cash value that builds within the life insurance can be used for any reason at any time, including investing. The cash value of whole life insurance is guaranteed to exceed the premiums paid, which means that means a person owning whole life insurance can eventually access and invest all premiums that they pay into the policy over time. After understanding that, the only argument that a person could possibly have is that a person "buying term and investing the difference" could have more money go into investments early on versus the person with whole life insurance. That may be true.

However, is it worth having slightly more money in investments if ultimately you are forced to self-insure? Does the difference in the investments make up for the cost of self-insuring? The answer is an emphatic NO WAY! If you are uncertain about this, reread Chapter 7.

What makes whole life insurance such a great tool? It fits perfectly well into the Velocity of Money strategy for wealth building and is the most effective way to own life insurance over time. Why? Because you maintain control and use of your money throughout your lifetime. Additionally, you pick up a combination of benefits that you cannot get from any other single financial product. Here are a few of the additional benefits:

1) You never lose the death benefit, and you own it over time. No other life insurance policy can boast about that. The death benefit represents future income, either from your earnings or your assets. If a person dies at any point along the way, the death benefit of the policy acts like a self-completion of what that person would have created had he/she lived.

2) You get disability protection on the contribution (called Waiver of Premium). Whenever a person becomes disabled, they lose their ability to earn income, and even if they have disability insurance, they only receive a portion (60% or so) of their pre-disability income. Expenses increase when a person becomes disabled. Something must give, and that something is usually savings and investing. It ends. When a person saves their money through whole life insurance with Waiver of Premium, their savings automatically continues when they become disabled. Life insurance is the only financial tool that offers disability protection on savings.

3) You can add an accelerated benefit rider to the policy that provides you cash from the policy's death benefit if you are terminally ill, chronically ill, or experience a critical illness (benefits that are often triggered by the same things that trigger benefits from a long-term care policy).

4) The ability to use your money in more than one place at the same time. How many banks will continue to pay you interest on money that you pull out and use to invest in something? Answer: None. When a person borrows money from their whole life insurance policy, they continue to earn interest on that same cash in their policy. No other financial tool gives you that ability.

What is the rate of return when you use your cash value to invest in other things? It is infinite. When a person borrows against the cash value of their whole life insurance, they are not actually withdrawing their money. Where is their money? It's still in the gross cash value of their life insurance earning at least 4% per year. Who's money is the person using then when they take a cash value loan? The insurance company's. Whatever rate of return the policyowner gets from the use of the cash value, it is actually infinite. Interestingly, this is what financial institutions do as well. They get an infinite return, because they don't invest their money, they invest yours. Whole life insurance is a uniquely powerful tool because it gives the policy owner the ability to get infinite rates of return, just like financial institutions.

5) The cash within the account grows tax-free (unless surrendered or the policy becomes a Modified Endowment Contract) and can be used tax-free (through policy loans) at any time for any reason. Policy loans should eventually be paid back to avoid causing the policy to cancel. Some may look at that as a false benefit because they say, "how is it my money if I have to pay it back?" You do not have to pay it back. If you do not pay it back the policy may eventually lapse, and the cash value above and beyond what you paid in premium will be taxable, just like any other savings account. However, the amazing part is that if you do pay the policy loan back, the insurance company will credit interest to your cash value in such a way that it looks like you never touched it. What other financial institution will do that for you? The fact that you can borrow cash value from your policy is not a problem, it is a benefit.

Imagine if I were a real estate investor. Typically, a real estate investor will save money in a bank account (liquid, guaranteed, accessible). This is money they are going to use as down payments on properties. Let's say I find a property and the required down payment is $100,000. I would then withdraw the $100,000 from the bank account and make the down payment. When I do that, is the bank going to continue paying me interest in the $100,000 I withdrew? No. Even if I eventually rebuild that $100,000? Will they pay me the interest I would have earned had I never taken it out? Of course not.

Now let's say I had the $100,000 in the cash value of my life insurance instead. If I take a policy loan out to make the down payment on a property, I am still going to earn interest on the full $100,000. Does the cash value loan have an interest that I have to pay to the insurance company? Yes. However, the better policies are going to credit most if not all the interest you pay back to your policy. So, no real loss there. Plus the difference between the interest you pay on a policy loan and the interest the insurance company credits to your account because of the interest payment, if any, is significantly less than I would have lost in taxes caused by a taxable savings account plus the cost of term life insurance premiums.

In my opinion whole life insurance is the most tax advantaged and most useful single financial product available. It has been around longer than almost any other current financial product. It has endured the test of time, depressions, recessions, and world wars. It is predictable. It is contractual. It is insurance on your income and insurance on your assets.

Robert Kiyosaki states in his book *Who Took My Money*, "Most people think investing is risky. It's not investing that is risky. Investing without insurance is risky." Having whole life insurance is not a guarantee of success, nor is it a guaranteed against failure. However, it certainly enhances your chances of success, and provides you with an invaluable tool to use in your progress to financial freedom.

Chapter 18: The Three Rules for Investing

Everyone wants to know, "where should I invest?" The problem is that's not the right question. Where you invest has much less to do with the success of your money than how you invest. Think of it this way: it's generally not the golf club that makes a person a great or terrible golfer. It's the swing. It's how the club is used. Therein lies the key to investing, it's "the how."

Why do people want to just know where to invest? Because "where" is easy. There are countless "where's" where a person can invest. In fact, there are new ones being created all the time: new businesses, new technologies, new inventions, new tax-favored products, new tax-favored non-product types of investments and new schemes. Things are changing all the time. It's the one constant. When I say "where" is easy, I'm saying that people want the easy path. They want me to tell them where they should put their money, versus trying to figure it out for themselves.

One industry (the financial services industry) in particular has risen to this desire for ease. Wall Street. They have "come to the rescue" for those wanting the easy path. They have made it extremely easy to "invest", through mutual funds, through 401(k)'s, IRA's, Health Savings Accounts, and various other ways. Contrary to other investing strategies, investing in the stock market is extremely easy and convenient.

Even Peter Lynch, the famous former Fund Manager of the Fidelity Magellan Fund said, "You shouldn't be intimidated. Everyone can do well in the stock market. You have the skills. You have the intelligence. It doesn't require any education. All you have to have is patience. Do a little research. You've got it!" (The Retirement Gamble, PBS Frontline Documentary).

Really? If you want to invest in the stock market you are basically born with the skills? You don't need "any" education? Do a little research?

Contrast that statement with this one from the book *Principles*, by Ray Dallio:

"The brilliant trader and investor Bernard Baruch put it well when he said, 'If you are ready to give up everything else and study the whole industry and background of the market and all the principal companies whose stocks are on the board as carefully as a medical student studies anatomy - if you can do all that and in addition you have the cool nerves of a gambler, the sixth sense of a clairvoyant and the courage of a lion, you have a ghost of a chance.'"

Here's the truth, investing, at least successful investing, requires expertise, hard work, a lot of time and effort, and generally a lot of money. True investing is a hard sale because it really isn't easy. Becoming at expert at anything requires dedication, time, effort, and knowledge.

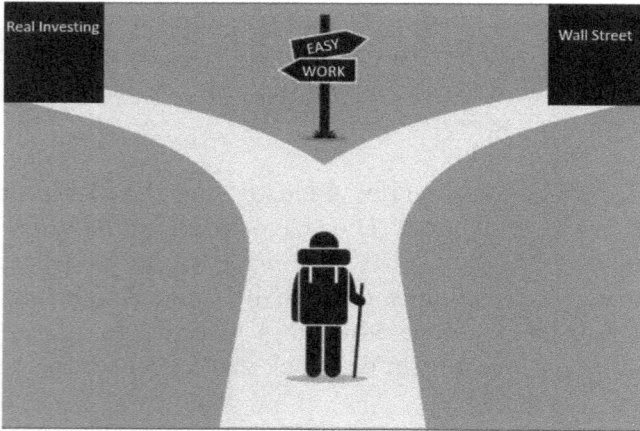

Where you should invest is something different for every client. It's something they have to figure out. There is no easy path to financial freedom. Robert Kiyosaki states in his book, *Rich Dad's Guide to Investing*, "One of the most important lessons I learned from my rich dad was that 'Investing is a plan, not a product or a procedure.'"

Peter Lynch's statement that all you need is "a little patience" is hogwash. But that's what Wall Street is selling, a huge lie.

Something that I have learned is that the best investments in the world require hard work, a lot of time and effort, and generally a lot

126

of money ("cash is king"). The worst investments require little cash, very little time and effort, and little to no work.

The worst investments are heavily marketed to the masses. There is a lot of advertising for them. The worst investments come in an extremely nice "wrapper." They are convenient and require no patience or knowledge. Based on that, investing in Wall Street is "easy" and "everyone can do it". However, investing this way, investing in the worst investments, is a loser's game. Robert Kiyosaki calls those types of investments "fake assets."

If you want to know how the most successful people became great at investing, read their autobiographies or read the research that has been done over time about successful people. Books such as *Think and Grow Rich*, by Napoleon Hill. Napoleon Hill compiled 20 years' worth of research about the most successful people in the world who lived at that time, including people such as JP Morgan, Andrew Carnegie, Henry Ford, and Charles Schwab.

It is estimated that Andrew Carnegie's net worth, at its height, was in the range of three hundred billion dollars. By comparison, today's wealthiest individual is Jeff Bezos (Amazon) at $113 billion. Andrew Carnegie was three times richer. Don't you think that Napoleon Hill's book has some important information about successful investing? Do you know what he doesn't talk about in his book? Where to invest the money. He teaches you how the most successful people in the world became that way.

Another great book to read on the subject is Thomas Stanley's (PhD) book, The Millionaire Next Door and its successor, *The Millionaire Mind*. Thomas Stanley interviewed thousands of millionaires in the United States over a period of twenty-five years. He found out a lot of interesting things about millionaires. You wouldn't recognize a millionaire as being such, because most millionaires don't flash their wealth. They shop at places like JC Penney. They drive American-made cars. Most are married. They are frugal (especially their spouses). As it relates to investing, he found that most did not credit Wall Street with their financial success. What did he find? He found that they invested in themselves, their professions, their own business, and their own property.

As we study these great books full of valuable information we find principles that we too can follow. Do people really think that those principles, the ones that Napoleon Hill wrote about so long ago, are outdated, and not applicable today? Are we supposed to throw those out and follow these new so-called principles of "dollar-cost averaging" into the stock market, a place where most millionaires in the past did not credit their success? Did that suddenly change? Is it because there are so many more "helpers," as Warren Buffet likes to call them, sharing in the stock market return piece of the pie? Of course not! It's the exact opposite. Is time, effort, and work an antiquated way of wealth, and now you just need "a little patience?" Of course not!

As I have studied, researched, and experienced myself, the same principles of wealth-building apply today that applied back when Andrew Carnegie was building his fortune. I summarize these principles into three "Rules." I call them rules because when someone breaks a rule, they are penalized. Such is true with investing. If you break these rules, you will pay a heavy price, eventually.

Rule #1 – Invest in Yourself
Is "diversification" really the best strategy for creating wealth? No, specialization is. Becoming an expert at something is. Think of the medical world. Who gets paid more, the general practitioner or the specialist? There's no question – it is the specialist. How could it be right in that situation, but not when it comes to other investments?

Specialized knowledge is a key to wealth creation and always has been. That being

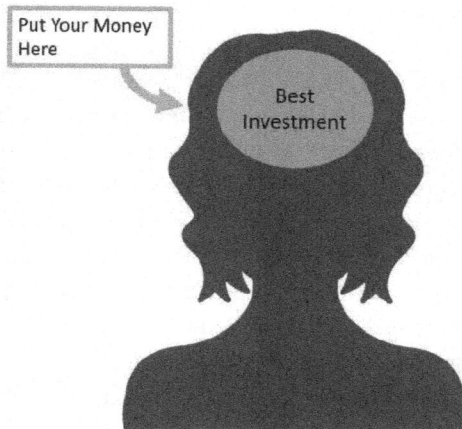

Put Your Money Here

Best Investment

the case, your best and first investment is YOU.

If you are interested in becoming a great real estate investor, for example, what should you do? Should you first hire a realtor and have them find property for you to buy? No. Without you taking the time to learn about real estate investing yourself, you have no way of knowing whether the property being presented to you is a good opportunity or not. You need to learn first, save money second (build up your liquidity), third, make sure your protection is right, and then invest. Invest time and money in learning. Read books, go to seminars and symposiums. Find a mentor (probably the best thing you can do).

Here is something easy to understand. We could have two people that own the same exact property or the same exact business, and the results of that property investment or that business investment could be completely different. It's not where you put your money, it's how. You are the investment, no matter where you put your money.

Rule #2 – Invest in What You Control
If you learn anything from highly successful people, you will learn that control of their business and assets was one of the biggest keys to their success. Let me ask you this. If you buy Wal-Mart stock, how much control do you have over the performance of that stock? Whatever it is, it's close to zero, nada, zilch. You could spend your entire paycheck every month at Wal-Mart and you won't move the needle at all. There's practically nothing you can do to influence how well Wal-Mart stock does. Whether the value goes up or down, whether the dividends are higher or lower, is completely out of your control. It is a boat in the ocean with no rudder. The only thing you can do is either buy more stock or sell it.

That's not how highly successful people invest. They invest in things they control. You might say, "well there isn't anything you can control 100%." I agree. But the scale isn't 0% or 100% control. There is also the entire range in between. Just because I can't control something 100% doesn't mean I shouldn't invest in assets where I have a much higher level of control than 0%.

129

Most people really do believe that investing means giving up control. That's not investing. Remember, investing means "covering completely".

Giving up control of your money is exactly what financial institutions want you to do, but it's the last thing they want to do. When a bank lends you money to buy a house, they tell you how much of a down payment you have to have. They tell you how much liquidity you have to have. They make you buy primary mortgage insurance (to protect them, not you). They make you buy "full replacement cost" coverage homeowners insurance. They don't give up all of their control. In fact, if you don't pay them as agreed, they take the house back.

Giving up control, whether it's in the stock market, a private placement offering, a REIT, or anything else, is begging for loss. Only you care about your money as much as you do. Only you know how much work you put forth to get your money. Don't give up control so easily. Retain as much control as possible.

Why do people want to give up control? Because it's easy. It gives them someone to blame other than themselves if the investment doesn't work out. When people give up control, they don't need to know anything. Again, it's a recipe for disaster, and is opposite of what actually creates wealth.

Why does the financial services industry encourage people to give up control of their money? Because that's what the financial institutions they work for want them to do. It's part of the Accumulation Theory of wealth building, and it doesn't work. It doesn't work because it goes against the principals that all financially successful people know and do. Control is a major key to success.

Rule #3 – Don't Chase Returns
When most people invest, how do they choose the investments they are going to put their money into? In most cases their decision is almost entirely based on projected or "historical" rates of return. Outside of that, they know almost nothing. What's wrong with that?

Well, we've already proven that averages mean nothing by themselves and can be very misleading (see Chapter 6).

Is it possible that the people running the investments themselves know that people really don't do any research, and that they base their decisions almost entirely on "average rates of return?" You bet they do! In other words, rates of return and projections are simply marketing. If you have read "the fine print" of any proforma or prospectus you will know that they all state something to this affect: "Past returns are no indication of future results. This investment is not guaranteed and you can lose money."

I would recommend you watch the movie *The Polka King*, with Jack Black. It's a great movie based on one of the strangest Ponzi schemes in US history. You'll find yourself thinking, "Why would people be dumb enough to invest their money with this guy? They don't know anything about the actual investment. They don't do anything to find out where the money is really going. How could they just hand over check after check to this guy?" The answer is, Jan Lewan, the real-life perpetrator of the scheme, promised them a rate of return, and they trusted him. That's it. That's all they knew. They gave up control. They gave up expertise, all because of the promised rates of return.

Of course this is a recipe for failure, but how many people realize that they are doing exactly the same thing with their retirement accounts, mutual funds, or other investments people propose to them? How do they choose the funds they are going to put their money into? They look at the marketing material conveniently supplied by the mutual funds/investment companies themselves, where they show average historical rates of return. When a person reviews those they choose to invest in the ones that did the best last year, for the past two years, for the past three years, or they choose the ones that project the highest rates of return. They almost never choose the funds that did poorly last year or for the past two years, even though it's almost guaranteed that last year's top performers won't be this year's top performers. Most investors do nothing else to "research" their investments. They spend about as much time figuring out which funds to put there money into as they would choosing which soda pop to buy out of a vending machine.

Consider these facts, taken from the book *The Smartest Investment Book You'll Ever Read*, by Daniel R. Solin: "An Exhaustive study of the performance record of funds rated "five stars" by Morningstar failed to find reliable statistical evidence that these funds performed any better than funds rated four stars or even three stars. The study also found that Morningstar ratings did only marginally better than other, far more simplistic, predictors of future performance."

In more than twenty years working with people who have money invested in mutual funds, I have not met with one person who could tell me even the name of any mutual fund manager where they had money invested. Not one! Don't you think that would be the minimum bit of knowledge a person should know? Even more important than last year's average rate of return? Looking at rates of return is not research. It is not investing.

Picking investments based on past performance alone is a loser's game. Using projected or historical rates of return as the basis, the main reason, for investing in something is begging for losses. Giving up control, expertise, and chasing returns is a sure bet for eventual failure.

By following and teaching these three rules for investing, you will save yourself and your clients all kinds of heartache in the future. I am not saying that if you or they follow these rules no money will ever be lost. Investing always has risk of loss. In fact, I know of no successful person that has never experienced loss. However, following these three rules will help minimize the loss and maximize the gain.

Your job, as the advisor, is not to pick the investments for your clients. It is to help them be positioned so that they are able to take advantage of whatever investment they choose to pursue. Your job is to help them know the difference between an Asset and a Liability. Your job is to help them learn how to be successful at saving money. Your job is to help them know how they can best protect their income and their assets. Your job is to help them reduce and recapture costs, not introduce new ones. Your job is to help them understand how money works and how to become a real investor.

Conclusion

To borrow a phrase from the Bible, "by their fruits ye shall know them". Financial Needs Analysis (FNA) and its companion, the Accumulation Theory, have been around long enough to see the fruits. Nearly every financial institution and the majority of financial professionals support it, but what has it produced? Do we have record financial independence in America or is it just the opposite, record dependence on government welfare? Either the constant promotion of Financial Needs Analysis has been unmotivating to people and they have not followed it, or they have followed it and it didn't work. Either way, it has failed.

According to the 2019 Retirement Confidence Survey (RCS) by the Employee Benefit Research Institute and Greenwald & Associates, "8 in 10 workers think they will work for pay in retirement." This means that most workers who are preparing for retirement, saving generally through IRA's and 401(k) plans, feel that they won't have enough money in those accounts to avoid having to work for income in retirement. Based on the report, currently 28% of retirees depend on working as a source of income in retirement.

What this does not tell us is how many retirees cannot work if they wanted to, due to health constraints. My guess is that if those numbers were included, we would see a clearer picture of how dire the real situation is for most retirees in America. The report admits such a probability as it states, "More than 4 in 10 retirees retired earlier than expected – most often because of a health problem or disability or changes within their organization" (in other words, they were replaced by younger, lower wage employees).

Additional findings in the RCS show that only 23% of workers feel "very confident" that they have enough money to live comfortably throughout retirement. At the same time, 59% of retirees stated that Social Security was "a major source of income" in retirement. Translated, 59% of Americans who are retired are totally dependent on the government for their income. SCARY! An additional 29% of retirees stated that Social Security was a minor source of income.

What we don't know is what percentage of that group followed the Velocity of Money Method for Wealth Creation and what percentage followed the Accumulation Theory. If the financial planning industry is an indication of the split, significantly more have tried to follow the Accumulation Theory. Easily more than nine out of ten financial advisors subscribe to, teach, and promote the Accumulation Theory and Needs-Based Planning.

However, we can see the statistics on how much wealth has been accumulated in 401(k)'s and IRA's and then calculate for ourselves how much income those amounts could possibly produce in today's financial environment. We point out those statistics in Chapter 15. As a reminder, for Americans in the 60-69 age range, the median 401(k) balance is $62,000. Pitiful.

FNA has not "worked" for the average American. Americans are underinsured, have not saved enough, do not have large enough balances in their investment and retirement accounts to replace their income, and are saddled with debt.

The Accumulation Theorists' response? People just need to save more, work longer, invest more, take more risk in the stock market (and keep money in the stock market at older and older ages) and continue to follow the same plan that has been promoted by financial institutions for the past fifty years. It has not worked!

Even the original creator of the principal financial tool of the Accumulation Method, the 401(k), has denounced the plan, saying it has turned into a "monster" (CBS News, 401(k) Founder: My Creation is "a monster", November 29, 2011).

In *The Great 401(k) Hoax*, written by William Wolman and Anne Colamosca, the authors explain, "The inability of the average American family to build a retirement nest egg during a stock market boom implies that the capital gains game envisioned by 401(k) proponents has all the makings of a Ponzi scheme. The chain letter phenomenon central to the machinations of the famed Bostonian, Charles Ponzi, was a fraud, pure and simple. Victims could, and did, call the cops, and the original improper Bostonian ended up in the

Bastille. No such easy outcome is open to those depending on the 401(k). As Yale University economist Robert J Shiller has observed, the unrealistic expectations that were built up about the financial returns promised by the 401(k) represent what is in effect an innocent fraud, the product of 'a naturally occurring Ponzi process.'"

On its face, Wall Street has devised a plan to "help" every American by giving easy access and ability to invest in a game that used to be played only by the wealthy. Wall Street did so by lobbying to replace the traditional defined benefit pension plan, which had a high level of restrictions on how and where the funds could be invested, with the defined contribution plan (401(k), IRA, SIMPLE, etc.), which has virtually no restrictions on where and how the money can be invested. One of the few restrictions for where those funds can be invested is not surprising. The funds in qualified plans can't be invested in life insurance, and until just recently, could not be invested in annuities. You don't have to be a genius to know why that is.

The Wall Street lobby had its greatest success when the Employee Retirement Income Security Act (ERISA) passed in 1974. Of course, business owners have been happy to shed the costly responsibilities and obligations of the defined benefit pension in favor of a new type of plan that has almost no obligation and absolutely no guarantee to the employee.

Outside of government organizations, very few defined benefit pension plans exist today. Most of the Wall Street proponents will say that the extinction of the defined benefit pension plan has been "an unintended consequence," but I believe it was completely intentional.

Can you imagine how Wall Street executives must have drooled over the money that was being poured into pension plans for decades prior to the passing of ERISA, as well as the prospect of contributions from millions of people who normally would NEVER have put a dime into the market on their own? Even the name of the act, which implies greater security to employees, is a fraudulent statement. It would have been more rightly called the Employee

Retirement Income Insecurity Act, and I believe it was all very intentional.

Since then there have been other lobbying victories for Wall Street, including the recent DOL rule that was passed in 2016, and the repeal of the Glass-Steagall Act in 1999, which previously made it illegal for banks to own subsidiary investment brokerages. Today almost all banking institutions and insurance companies have a subsidiary securities brokerage attached. This connection had a huge role in causing the Great Recession in 2008 (the connection and joint profiteering generated from sketchy loans and the inventions of the investment banking world – Collateralized Debt Obligations – CDO's). If you don't believe me, watch the documentary *Inside Job*, by Charles Ferguson. Who lost in that deal? Certainly not the banks or investment brokerages. The loser was the poor person with a 401(k) and IRA.

From the early 70's was born the Financial Needs Analysis (FNA) approach to financial planning, because prior to that time, people were either entrepreneurs and already investing mainly in themselves, their own ideas, and their own property, or they worked for a company that provided them with guaranteed income for the rest of their lives after retiring. People did not have to depend nearly as much on their own ability to invest as they do today. Unfortunately, FNA has only encouraged people to do exactly what Wall Street executives want them to do; give them their money, on a regular and ongoing basis, give up control and expertise, and give back as little as possible. The victims of this scheme are the average American. They are being sold a lie that they can save a few bucks a month and with the miracle of compounding interest, they too can retire, maybe even early.

The incredible level of dependence on Social Security Retirement Income, which was never designed to be a major source of retirement income, is now the chief source for most retirees. Government dependence is at an all-time high. It is unsustainable and it is breaking the financial back of our country. When Social Security Retirement benefits were first introduced in 1935, the average lifespan of an American male was 59.9 years and female was 63.9 years. According to the Social Security Administration website, "the new Act created a social insurance program designed to pay retired workers age 65 or older a continuing income after retirement."

Putting two and two together, it's obvious that Social Security Retirement benefits weren't going to be for everyone, as most would die prior to becoming eligible to receive it at that time, and those that did live long enough to receive it weren't going to receive it for very long.

Today, the average American is expected to live to age 78.6, according to the Centers for Disease Control and Prevention. Additionally, the amount of money being collected from the American workforce is not sufficient to pay the current promised benefits to retirees. According to the "Fast Facts & Figures About Social Security, 2018" chartbook, created by the Social Security Administration itself, slightly more than $1 trillion was collected through Social Security taxes, and slightly more than $1 trillion was paid out. 2018 marked the first year in the SSA's history where more money was paid out than was collected, by about $1.7 billion. Unfortunately, this scenario is only going to worsen, unless big changes take place in the realm of entitlement and welfare, and the way the financial services industry provides advice to the public. The amount of pressure the failed philosophy of Financial Needs Analysis and the Accumulation Theory is putting on Social Security is at epidemic proportions.

It's time for a revolution in the planning industry. It's time for a whole new approach and philosophy, one that utilizes economic principles, one that teaches people how to create wealth, as financial institutions do, instead of simply promoting what financial institutions want people to do. It's time for planners to promote financial literacy instead of financial dependence. It's time for Americans to go back to depending on themselves, their own innovation, their own expertise, and their own entrepreneurship. America was and still is the land of opportunity, but most have been lulled into dependence on Wall Street and the Government. We've got to turn this ship around. By teaching the principles in this book, you can do your part and you can make a difference to your clients. Your clients can avoid being one more Financial Needs Analysis and Accumulation Theory casualty.

It's up to you as the advisor. If you want to follow the crowd, then Principles-Based Planning isn't for you. The crowd is going to follow the financial institution lobby. If you want to do what's popular, Principles-Based Planning and Velocity of Money isn't for you. If you don't mind being alone, alone at the top, with your clients, then this is the method that has proven to work throughout history. My challenge for you is to avoid taking the easy path. Don't be afraid of going against the grain. Teach your clients what really works and by so doing, you and your clients can achieve true financial independence.

ABOUT THE AUTHOR

Kyle began working in the financial services industry in 1999 and started his own financial planning practice in 2004. Kyle's practice is focused on helping clients become financially free.

Kyle is also the creator of Personal Financial Snapshot™, a principles-based planning system. His purpose with the software is to help change how the industry does financial planning.

Kyle is a CERTIFIED FINANCIAL PLANNER™ professional (CFP®).

Kyle lives in Texas with his wife and children.

Kyle J Christensen, CFP®

Made in USA - Kendallville, IN
1161715_9798665132310
12.26.2020 1501